From the Frontline

From the Frontline of History

From the Frontline of History

Also by Nick Bastin:

A Very Canny Scot, Daniel Campbell of Shawfield and Islay (with Joanna Hill)

BloodBond

BloodFeud

BloodLine

From the Frontline of History

Teddy Campion at war with the Seaforth Highlanders

1895 - 1916

Nick Bastin

From the Frontline of History

Copyright © 2022 by Nick Bastin All rights reserved

The moral right of the author has been asserted

ISBN: 9798846485419

No part of this publication may be reproduced, stored in a retrieval system, or transmitted in any form or by any means, electronic, mechanical, photocopying, recording, scanning, or otherwise, without the prior written permission of the author.

From the Frontline of History

Acknowledgements

This has been a long term and fascinating project to work on. It started in 2016 when my Aunt Carolyn Countess Fortescue loaned me Teddy's Boer War diary. I was immediately captivated by the writer's personality and set out to find out more about him. Without her loan of the diary this book would not exist.

There are so many others to thank too. In particular, I would like to thank my distant cousins Jill Hewitt and Will Campion for the loan of Teddy's Sudan Diary, and Sarah Campion for connecting us; Cameron Shenton for the use of some of his photographs, and Christopher Mellor-Hill at Noonans of Mayfair for helping me to track him down; The Highlanders Museum at Fort George for all their support and their excellent archive, and in particular Robert Shanks for his invaluable photography research; Major Maurice Gibson for his enthusiasm and hospitality; Calum Robertson, Margaret Wilson and Vicky Brown at the Scottish National War Museum for all their help with the Egerton Archive; Dominic Hoole for his information on the death of Charles Campion; the staff of the Templar Study Centre at the National Army Museum, London, and the Keep Archive, Brighton; Lee Smart for the use of his map of the retreat from Le Cateau; Dr Craig Goldsack of University College London Hospitals for his perspective on Teddy's cause of death; Richard Burrows of Danny for all his help; and Simon Vickers and Matt Mackenzie at Lyon & Turnbull.

From the Frontline of History

My particular thanks to Alan MacDonald for putting me in touch with Colonel (Retired) James Hopkinson OBE who so kindly agreed to write the foreword. James has impeccable Seaforth connections, with his grandfather serving under Teddy on the Western Front and eventually taking over command. I can think of no one more fitting to write the foreword and I am very grateful for his time and wisdom.

I want to thank my wife Mairi for her efforts in proof reading my terrible grammar, any remaining comma splices are all my own work; and my son Lachlan for helping to track down photos in the National War Museum.

Finally, I want to thank Teddy for taking me on such an interesting journey over 100 years after his death. As my Great Grandmother's brother, he was always likely to have been long dead before I could ever have known him, but I have come to appreciate his company and especially his humour and courage.

Contents

Acknowledgements	5
Foreword	8
Introduction	13
Prologue	19
Teddy's Early Life	21
Teddy's Family	26
Teddy Joins Up	31
The Crete Crisis of 1897	36
The Sudan Campaign	59
The Legacy of the Sudan Campaign	92
Return to Active Service and the Boer War	100
Between Wars in India and Scotland	134
Teddy and The Great War	155
The Battles of the Marne and Aisne	170
In Flanders Fields	188
The Second Battle of Ypres	219
Return to the Front	234
Funeral	246
Epilogue	250
Conclusion	254

From the Frontline of History

Foreword

In April this year I was driving through the middle of Bristol when my phone rang. It was an old friend, Alan MacDonald, who said that a friend of his, Nick Bastin, with regimental connections to the Seaforth Highlanders had just written a book about the war diaries of his great, great uncle, Lieutenant Colonel Teddy Campion. Nick was looking for someone to write the foreword and Alan had thought of me. Why me?

Well, I suppose on two counts: firstly, that I had been a soldier for twenty-odd years and had commanded The Highlanders, whose antecedents were the Seaforth Highlanders; but secondly and more importantly, my grandfather, John Hopkinson, had been a contemporary of Teddy Campion and took over battalion command of 2nd Seaforth on 6th May 1915 after Teddy was badly gassed. My grandfather was the only remaining Captain left in the Battalion when he assumed command. His career mirrored much of Teddy's and therefore it was particularly interesting to read such a personal account. I was delighted to be asked to write this foreword to Nick's excellent biography of Teddy Campion.

There are many books and accounts covering the period before and during the First World War but few span as full career as Teddy's or give such a personal insight to the many campaigns and theatres where he saw service. From a personal perspective, I was fascinated to read this book as both a soldier but also to understand what my grandfather went through given the paucity of his personal family papers.

Up until the First World War, Teddy, like many of the regulars from that generation, had enjoyed a career of Imperial soldiering with skirmishes and small bush wars across what was then the British Empire. He bounced from Crete to the Sudan, to South Africa, then to India before facing the rigours of the trenches in Flanders. In contrast, my grandfather, joining slightly later in 1900, being four years younger, missed South Africa and found himself kicking his heels in Cairo. Like most soldiers seeking adventure he transferred to The King's Africa Rifles and managed to get on operations against the 'Mad Mullah' in Somaliland, fighting at Jidbali. My grandfather returned to 2nd Seaforth in 1907 in Aldershot before requesting service in the West African Frontier Force where he stayed until war broke out in 1914. He hurriedly rejoined 2nd Seaforth on 5th September as part of a batch of reinforcements, joining A Company, Teddy's company, where he remained until 1915. This included the memorable Christmas truce in 1914 where both adversaries met in No Man's Land on Christmas Eve and Day.

Teddy Campion took part with 2nd Seaforth in the 2nd Battle of Ypres in late April 1915 and assumed command of 2nd Seaforth following the wounding of the Commanding Officer and the death of the Senior Major, whilst my grandfather took over command of A Company. My grandfather had only just returned to the Battalion on 19th April having been admitted to hospital in March with exhaustion and pneumonia. The 2nd Battle of Ypres marked the first appalling mass use of chlorine gas, which was to impact many of those who served on the Western Front and resulted ultimately in Teddy's death on 25th February 1916 at the age of 42. By 6th May 1915, my grandfather had temporarily taken over command of 2nd Seaforth when Teddy was admitted to hospital following an earlier gas attack. Teddy Campion returned to command in September 1915 until November before being hospitalised for gastritis.

As a former soldier there are several aspects of these diaries that fascinated me, many of which ring true to this day. The Imperial Army of Teddy's day attracted those seeking a life of service, adventure and travel; it still does. Until the First World War, his career was one of interesting colonial wars interspersed with periods of organised enjoyment and boredom. Teddy was a career soldier who had sought the Army as a profession. His early diary entries are all too reminiscent of those of junior officers – the incompetence of those above them foremost amongst them! It was ever thus. By the start of the First World War, Teddy was a hard-bitten, experienced professional officer. He was a company commander and relatively old at 40. The entries reflect the serious nature of life; gone are the care-free thoughts of the young immortal man. It was a tough dangerous life, where living in the trenches took its toll on all as much from the weather as enemy action, especially in 1914. Comparing kit and equipment between now and then is remarkable; wool that quickly became sodden when wet, few decent waterproofs unless privately bought, and heavy kilts in which to fight and respirators that didn't work. No Gore-Tex, no combat body armour, and no windproof wicking materials. Soldiering is a young person's game, so being 40 years old would have been doubly hard – both

From the Frontline of History

Teddy and my grandfather were hospitalised from exhaustion/pneumonia on a number of occasions.

Even Imperial policing operations carried a constant stream of attrition either through disease, accident or direct enemy action. The First World War entries really bring this home when you look at Teddy and my grandfather's appointments; company second in command to temporary command of a battalion all in less than nine months. My grandfather was hospitalised once for exhaustion and wounded three times, twice seriously, both from indirect shellfire. Teddy similarly was hospitalised twice due to exhaustion/pneumonia and twice more from the effects of having been gassed. Casualties, constant turnover of men with battle casualty replacements became everyday occurrences and are treated in the official war diaries as very matter of fact hiding their corrosive nature on fighting spirit. The nadir being the first day of the Battle of the Somme, 1st July 1916, when 2nd Seaforth suffered 450 casualties, including 17 Officers killed, leaving just three Officers and eighty Other Ranks by 2nd July. What is extraordinary, is that despite those numbers of casualties, battalions like 2nd Seaforth never wavered and never broke, due in large measure to the toughness of the Jocks and the steadfast leadership at both Non-Commissioned Officer and Commissioned Officer levels. Nowhere is this better epitomised than Teddy's order to 2nd Seaforth:

From the Frontline of History

"Remember, no Seaforth Highlander ever has left, or ever will leave, his post. Whatever damnable engine of war the enemy use, the Seaforths will stick it out and will have their reward in killing the enemy."

This in the face of a gas attack.

I like to think that this steadfast battle discipline endures today as warranted by the bravery of so many British soldiers, men and women, during the recent conflicts in Iraq and Afghanistan. Worthy descendants of an earlier extraordinary generation.

Colonel (Retired) JMR Hopkinson OBE

From the Frontline of History

Introduction

Edward "Teddy" Campion was a child of his class and of his time. Born into a privileged, aristocratic family in the late-Victorian era, he grew up as part of a society that had a surprisingly global outlook. This was a time of Imperial expansion, of opportunity for members of his class, when a quarter of the world was coloured in pink, or so the Imperial maps would declare; an Empire where the sun never set. But as a younger son he would inherit nothing; he would have to make his own way in the world. He chose to become a soldier and spent twenty years campaigning with his regiment the Seaforth Highlanders, The Ross-shire Buffs: The Duke of Albany's.

While Teddy was certainly a brave and effective officer, no tales have come down to us of death-defying valour, nor single-handed defeats of overwhelming enemy forces; no Victoria Crosses were conferred. It is true that he was gazetted for valour on the field of battle, but so were many others. Instead, he rose steadily through the ranks, until in the crucible of the Western Front in World War One, he ultimately commanded the 2nd Battalion Seaforth Highlanders. This command would cost him his life.

Why should we be interested in Teddy today over a century after his death? The Empire is gone and many of the wars in which he fought are now seen in a different context: the context of colonialism, oppression and exploitation.

From the Frontline of History

What sets Teddy apart is that he was a great diarist, and from his earliest overseas service in the International Occupation of Crete until his death, he has left us a trail of diaries and letters that open up a window into that now long vanished world. Only a small part of this material has ever been published and it has never been contextualised in the life of the writer. In many ways, he is an exemplar of the late Victorian military career, conducted as the British Empire reached its zenith and started its inexorable decline.

The unusual breadth of his diaries, which cover a range of very varied conflicts, give us an insight into the thinking and attitudes of men like Teddy and his time. Much of his writing is strikingly modern and could easily be written by a soldier of today – particularly when bemoaning the actions of some superior officers. Of course, some of the attitudes are jarring to the modern ear. Without wanting to excuse them, I suspect they were very typical of their time.

The Sudan Diary and the Boer War Diary remain in family hands and have never been reproduced before. The Crete Diary, of which he was the major contributor, was retained by Granville Egerton, his commanding officer, and is now at the National Army Museum's archive. His letters have been drawn from both the Egerton Archive at the National War Museum in Edinburgh, and from the Campion family archive, known as the Danny Archive, held at the Keep Archive in Brighton. Many of the latter letters have been incorrectly attributed to his brother, William Robert Campion.

While Teddy generally has pretty good hand writing, the volume of material and some of the complex and unfamiliar names and terms (especially in Sudan and the Boer War) mean that I am likely to have made mistakes in transcription for which I can only apologise. Where something is utterly illegible I have marked it as such. All mistakes are my own.

There is undoubtedly a breezy self-confidence and underlying sense of mission throughout the diaries. For example, there is never any doubt expressed that marching deep into the Sudan to overthrow the Dervishes was anything other than a just mission. Certainly, the destruction he witnessed in the countryside, and the general impoverishment of the people, reflected, in his view, the evils of Dervish hegemony. It is perhaps worth noting that the Sudan campaign was conducted in conjunction with Egyptian and Sudanese forces, both of which he clearly admired. Similarly, the International Occupation of Crete was a peace keeping mission with striking similarities to those of the late 20th and early 21st centuries.

He describes the Battles of Atbara and Omdurman in great detail and perhaps they were the last of the "traditionally-fought" battles of the long 19th century. Atbara was a classic battle of the period, with an initial artillery bombardment of enemy positions, followed by an infantry advance to close quarters, and dispersal of the enemy at the point of a bayonet. Omdurman, by contrast, pitted the glorious if foolhardy courage of the Dervishes in a full-frontal cavalry charge over a plain, a plain which provided a perfect and deadly field of fire for the British Maxim guns and rifle fire. Despite the vastly superior numbers of the Dervishes, the outcome was never seriously in doubt.

From the Frontline of History

The contrast with the Boer War is profound. The Boers understood that set piece battles would not favour them and, after a few striking early successes, they instead relied increasingly on skirmishing and ambush to wear down their opponent. Much of Teddy's Boer War diary details the building and staffing of the chain of blockhouses that the British used to break up the Boers' freedom of movement. It was pretty dull work, for the most part.

He was also part of a striking innovation, the Mounted Infantry, to some degree inspired by the mobility of the Boer forces. This saw foot regiments using horses to move around and cover large distances swiftly. The Seaforths provided several companies of Mounted Infantry in the latter stages of the War and this development was much heralded at the time. As part of the 1st Battalion Seaforth Highlanders[1], Teddy was sent to South Africa relatively late in the war in 1901. For Teddy, there were certainly moments of jeopardy, but there were also games of polo to be played and trips into town to relax, quite a contrast to the boredom and oppressive heat of Sudan.

After the Boer War, there was a period of relative peace and calm when he was posted to India and was able to indulge his passions for sport of all kinds, and especially cricket and polo. He then transferred to Scotland, where he helped transform the Seaforths' Volunteer and Militia units into the 3rd Battalion Seaforth Highlanders who would play such a critical role in the war to come.

---

[1] The 2nd Seaforths had already been engaged and had suffered heavily at Magersfontein, where General Wauchope, the Commander of the 3rd (Highland) Brigade, and who Teddy had thought highly of in the Sudan, was killed along with many men.

From the Frontline of History

By the time Teddy saw action in the First World War, the nature of battle had changed entirely. Now, fighting against an equally powerful and well-equipped enemy, the unremitting brutality and remorseless nature of combat was immediately evident. Teddy's blood-curdling account of the retreat from Le Cateau in August 1914, during the very earliest days of the war, shows us that this would be entirely unlike the colonial wars of the past. Of course, with the benefit of hindsight, we know that the war went on for another four years and slaughtered millions, but the evidence was there from the earliest days, even if Teddy - like so many at the time - thought that it could all be over by Christmas.

His descriptions of trench warfare and house to house fighting are fresh and vivid and have never been reproduced before. While the story may be well known in generalities, it is a different thing altogether to read the day by day account from the Battalion War Diary and to calculate the losses of life and casualties, the massacre of a few minutes wiping out decades of friendships.

The losses are unimaginable today. Between April and May 1915, 95% of the Officers and 112% of the NCOs and men[2] of the 2nd Battalion Seaforth Highlanders were killed, missing or wounded. How can one begin to understand that?

The many familiar images of the First World War are all here: trenches, mud, poison gas, constant shelling and the threat of snipers, the freezing cold and

---

[2] 32 Officers and 961 NCOs and men of the 2nd Battalion Seaforth Highlanders were killed, missing, wounded or gassed between 1 April and 30 May 1915

relentless rain. The famous Christmas Truce of 1914, where a game of football was held between combatants, is also shown to not be quite all we are led to believe.

It is easy to find much to recoil from – the indiscriminate murder of fellow human beings, the thrill of bloodlust when its leash is slipped, the relentless numbers of casualties rising day after day, until an occasional bloodletting such as at Ypres II wipes the slate red. But there is also camaraderie and a sense of duty and commitment, almost beyond the bounds of sense or reason. More than a hundred years later, we can look back and experience that precarious existence at first hand in the mud and blood of Flanders fields. We can read it here and be grateful that we have not had to endure such hardships and hope that we will learn to never repeat the mistakes of the past.

From the Frontline of History

Prologue

It had been a fine day; the air was almost still except for a slight breeze from the north. Lieutenant-Colonel Edward 'Teddy' Campion looked out across the mud churned battlefield, trying to understand what was happening, or what was about to happen. His sentries in the furthermost trench had sent word that something very strange was afoot. German troopers were scurrying back and forth across their trench line; they would not normally expose themselves in this way. A few shells landed dispersing a peppery and irritating gas, but apart from that, nothing.

He moved to the observation point and looked out towards the German line. He'd heard the rumours, they'd all heard the rumours – of a deadly new weapon that the Germans had developed, a gas weapon that killed indiscriminately. The French and Canadians further up the line had been devastated by its effects only the week before. There were accounts of 6,000 men found dead, asphyxiated. Those that hadn't been killed had had their skin burned and their lungs scorched by the fumes.

A week before, too, the Battalion had suffered one of its gravest days of losses, not just of the war but in its entire history. They were thinly spread: something that the Germans would surely know, and that they would doubtless use to their advantage. If they broke through the line here there was no saying what damage they could do. The Germans hadn't mounted many offensives since the war had descended into the trenches – was this the moment for their big break through? After so many months of fighting, all through the winter in the freezing mud and snow, the Seaforths had helped to keep them at bay. But now, with so few men left, would they be able to hold the line?

He tore off an order paper and took out a pencil. What to write? He thought of all the letters he had been writing to the families of the men who'd died. More than half of the Battalion had been killed or wounded in the previous week alone; there were so few of them left. However, this was no time for great literature; his order needed to be as simple as possible without any complicated notions that could be obscured by the fog of war. Time was pressing. He wrote carefully but deliberately:

> *To Officer Commanding Company and men to see*
>
> *Remember, no Seaforth Highlander ever has left, or ever will leave, his post.*
>
> *Whatever damnable engine of war the enemy use, the Seaforths will stick it out and will have their reward in killing the enemy.*

He signed it and called over the trench runner to take it to the fire trench closest to the enemy. He returned to look out over the battlefield. A mist seemed to be gathering. It was late afternoon, too early for an evening fog. He stared at it. Minute by minute the mist thickened into a roiling, greenish-grey cloud that crept slowly but inexorably over no man's land towards them.

He gritted his teeth. They must hold the line.

From the Frontline of History

Chapter 1 — Teddy's early life

Edward Campion was born on 18 December 1873, the third and youngest son of Colonel William Henry Campion of Danny, West Sussex, and his wife Gertrude Brand, the daughter of the Right Honourable Sir Henry Bouverie Brand, 1st Viscount Hampden. Known as "Teddy" by all, he was part of a large close knit family, with three brothers and four younger sisters.

The Campions were an old, landed family, who had come to Danny from their estates at Combwell in Kent when in 1702 Henry Campion married Barbara Courthope, an heiress who had inherited Danny from her father's family. While clearly comfortably off, and with significant land holdings, they were by no means cash rich and the ever shrinking acreage speaks to regular sales of outlying holdings to keep the main estate going.

Teddy's father, Colonel William Henry Campion had served as a Captain in the 72nd Regiment, Duke of Albany's Own Highlanders, which was later merged with the 78th Highlanders Regiment of Foot in 1881 to create the 1st Battalion Seaforth Highlanders. He also served as Lieutenant Colonel, 2nd Volunteer Battalion, of the Royal Sussex Regiment. He had fought in the Crimea, where he was present at the Battle of the Great Redan at Sebastopol in 1855, and later in the suppression of the Indian Mutiny under General Colin Campbell.

Danny is a large Elizabethan 'E' house, built in 1593, just outside the town of Hurstpierpoint in West Sussex, and sheltering under the lee of Wolstonbury

From the Frontline of History

Hill on the South Downs. It is an idyllic setting, with an ancient park filled with huge oak trees that have seen the centuries come and go.

In Charles Phillimore's[3] account of life at Danny before the First World War[4], he describes the family thus:

> Life at Danny was extremely pleasant. The house was a centre for a large cousinhood and for many brothers and sisters. It was obviously the house of really religious people, but the religion was unostentatious and the atmosphere of happiness was everywhere….
>
> The old Squire was very fond of shooting and hunting and still an excellent shot….In his later years when his seat in the saddle had come to depend on balance rather than grip, he often "took a toss" hunting and thought nothing of it, but when he was thrown into a stream in which he was entirely submerged at the age of about 75, and had eight miles to ride home in mid-Winter, he was careful to change and mention nothing about it on his return. Mrs Campion, however, happened to see his clothes being taken away to be dried. When taxed with what had happened, he only said "If I haven't learnt to fall at my age I never shall….."
>
> No one was idle at Danny: Mrs Campion was always engaged in good works….I believe that in their youth her children had been frightened

---

[3] Charles Augustus Phillimore married Alice "Elsie" Campion, Teddy's younger sister, in 1908
[4] Danny Archive: DAN/1/13/490

of her, but all trace of that had gone by the time I knew her, and she was continually chaffed by all her children.

Teddy's mother, Gertrude, as Phillimore's passage asserts, was always doing good works, frequently visiting the sick or elderly fellow parishioners. She clearly had a fierce energy which drove her to establish charitable institutions, particularly those focused on the needs of women and young girls. Her obituary in the Mid Sussex Times in 1926 is stirring in its description of her achievements:

The deceased lady was the aunt of the present Viscount Hamden, a woman of striking personality and ability. Her kindness and readiness to helping charitable causes made her a general favourite throughout Sussex. Ever a champion of her sex, she did a great deal of exceedingly useful work for women and young girls and her efforts resulted in the founding of a number of valuable institutions. Among other things, she was the Foundress and President of the former Diocesan Training Home for Workhouse Girls which was established in June 1884 for the purpose of affording workhouse girls a proper training in domestic service. She was keenly interested in the Girls' Friendly Society, in which she was formally President. She also had a great deal to do with the founding of the Chichester Diocesan Purity Association and the Mothers Union, and was chiefly responsible for founding and nursing to success the Barclay Home for Blind Girls in Wellington Rd Brighton. Mrs Campion was also responsible for founding Sunshine Home, Hurstpierpoint, with the object to providing a convalescent home for women and girls. During the war it became a military hospital and in 1922 Mrs Campion handed it over to the Church Army.[5]

This energy must also have pervaded the home, and one can imagine that Gertrude was not one to foster indolence! Perhaps this fed into Teddy's diligence in keeping a diary. Presumably there were all sorts of reasons to be distracted at the end of a long day on campaign, and the effort of consistently writing up his entries would have required focus and resolve.

Into this house and family, Teddy was born and raised. It was clearly a cheerful and tightknit household although leavened with a sense of duty, respect and religion. The family enjoyed the benefits of the late-Victorian landed gentry's lifestyle: there was plenty of hunting and shooting, as well as a strong sense of religious duty and purpose. Teddy would need these attributes during his military career.

While Teddy grew up surrounded by the estates of his ancestors and in a wonderful home, he always knew that with two older brothers he had no prospect of inheriting. He would have to make his own way in the world; such is the lot of the younger son or daughter.

He clearly loved Danny, and occasionally refers to it in his diaries. On his return home from South Africa there is a particular poignancy at a moment when age and perspective have given the soldier a greater appreciation of home:

---

[5] Mid Sussex Times - 27 December 1927

Well done diary, the short time is over, the game played and your author now counting the days, nay the very hours, that bring him nearer the old home. The home of his ancestors, the home where he was born, the home he loves.

Perchance you may think it foolish of a soldier to hanker after home and all that it holds dear. Yet foolish or not the fact remains it is so; as we slowly grow to years of [some] discretion, be the amount small or great, the more when one leaves home to embark on some enterprise where danger lies does more one count up the chances for or against the likelihood of returning.

If Teddy were to visit the house today, he would find it little changed from the outside. The worn red brick and ancient trees would indeed be achingly familiar. Inside, some of the family pictures remain on the walls of the great hall and on the stairs. The building retains its warm and welcoming atmosphere, but the family is long gone.

Chapter 2   Teddy's Family

Teddy belonged to a large family of eight brothers and sisters. He was the third of four sons and was followed by four daughters. His older brothers trod their own path, with Bill, the eldest, unsuccessfully standing as an MP in two elections before being elected MP for Lewes between 1910 and 1924. He was also a member of the London Stock Exchange. Bill went on to have his own very distinguished military career with the Royal Sussex Yeomanry, later the Royal Sussex Regiment, which he commanded at Sulva Bay in Gallipoli in August 1915. After being wounded, he was evacuated back to England in October, but served again in France, ultimately leading the 4th Royal Sussex through the bloody 100 Days Campaign in 1918 that ended the war. He was awarded the Distinguished Service Order. Between 1924 and 1931, he was the Governor of Western Australia, a territory of 2.6 million square kilometres, equivalent to a third of Australia's land mass – clearly a position of considerable responsibility.

Teddy's next oldest brother Frederick, known as "Freddie", pursued an interesting path after travelling to Australia as the tutor to the children of the Governor, his uncle, Viscount Hampden. While he was there, he was inspired to bring the bible to the Aboriginal community and decided to train as a priest[6]. He later dedicated his life to this goal, founding the well-known Australian organisation the Brotherhood of the Good Shepherd – otherwise known as the

---

[6] Australian Dictionary of Biography, Volume 7, (MUP), 1979

Bush Brothers. He also served with his elder brother at Gallipoli as military Chaplain to the Royal Sussex Regiment.

Teddy's only younger brother, Charles Campion, known as "Charlie", was born on 17 December 1876, and would also follow him into military service. For reasons that are not clear, Charlie joined the Ceylon Mounted Infantry as a trooper and was posted to South Africa at the outset of the second Boer War in 1899[7]. It is possible that he had a distant cousin[8] among the founders of the Ceylon Mounted Infantry in the 1880s and his joining was prompted by that connection. The Ceylon Mounted Infantry saw action at Stinkhoutboom, Cape Colony, Driefontein, Johannesburg, Diamond Hill and Wittebergen, and were praised by General Kitchener who said:

> *The Ceylon Contingent did very good work in South Africa I only wish we had more of them.*[9]

At some point, Charlie transferred first to Brigadier-General Broadwood's Column and then to the police, where he was Superintendent at Pretoria. Finally, and fatefully, he joined the 69th Company Imperial Yeomanry as a Lieutenant and was killed at the Battle of Vlakfontein on 29 May 1901. There were horrific accounts of the Boers shooting wounded soldiers dead in cold blood after the battle, including Charlie who was reportedly shot in the head

---

[7] https://www.wikitree.com/wiki/Menzies-1963
[8] A Courthope is listed as among the founders of the unit in the 1880s, it was through a marriage to Barbara Courthope that the Campions had come to Danny in the 18th century
[9] https://www.wikiwand.com/en/Ceylon_Mounted_Rifles

while having a wound dressed. The Daily Mail, which broke the story, was threatened by the Government, with Kitchener threatening to have its access to casualty lists removed. The Government was presumably keen not to overly demonise the Boers who would inevitably be part of any peace discussions. However, the Daily Mail did not back down and this became a national scandal.

On 16 July 1901, more details of the story leaked out to the media, when 2nd Trooper E. Saddington of the Sussex Squadron, 7th Battalion Imperial Yeomanry wrote[10]:

> Lieutenant Campion, one of our officers, and a Sergeant of the Devonshire 27th Company Imperial Yeomanry, were murdered. Campion was shot through the finger; the Sergeant was binding it up when three Boers came up and blew their brains out.

This was quite a cover up, since the Government had known the story since at least 11 June and probably before. Many accusations have been flung back and forth and 120 years later it is hard to be definitive. What is inarguable is that Charles Campion died and there is no alternative account of his death other than his being shot in cold blood by a Boer.

His death caused his parents great sorrow, and they erected a large stained-glass window in his memory at Holy Trinity Church, Hurstpierpoint in 1902. Coming from such a close family, Charlie's death must also have made a profound impact on Teddy, and he marks the date of Charlie's birthday in

---

[10] Mid Sussex Times 16 July 1901

From the Frontline of History

December 1901 in his Boer War diary. While there is no intemperate talk of "revenge" it is hard to know whether or not Charlie's death contributed to his posting to South Africa. He does not seem to blame all Boers for the actions of some and one can imagine that as a long-term soldier he was already perfectly familiar with the consequences of war.

Teddy had three surviving sisters: Mary, Alice (known as "Elsie") and Joan[11], with Mary in particular a force to be reckoned with. She was very active with the British Red Cross, participating in the Voluntary Aid Detachment during World War One. Perhaps inspired by Teddy's death, Mary travelled to France and helped establish the Hostel for Relatives in the Hotel des Anglais at Le Touquet. The Hostel, which opened on July 4 1916, provided housing for the wives and near relatives who were allowed to visit patients in No.1 Red Cross Hospital, based in the Casino. This was important as all the hotels in Paris Plage and Le Touquet, with few exceptions, had been requisitioned as hospitals, so lodging was difficult to obtain, and exceedingly costly. Capacity was between 120 and 160 patients and visitors at any time, so it was a substantial operation. Mary ran it for three years until 1918 and is described thus:

> *Commandant Campion V.A.D. Sussex/84, has here won an undying reputation for kindliness, loyalty and a wonderful taste and sense of beauty. She helps the many relatives of seriously wounded Officers who*

---

[11] Teddy's oldest sister Bridget was born in 1875 but died in 1881

find a very warm welcome at the Hostel. Her Unit shows the very best spirit.[12]

Unquestionably, Teddy had grown up in a family very attuned to service, especially with the military. The contribution of the family over many years at the height of Britain's Empire is evident and must have been an inspiration as well as a considerable burden of expectation – not that he ever expresses it as such in his diaries. Nonetheless, the bitter seeds of the Empire's destruction were already being sown.

---

[12] http://www.scarletfinders.co.uk/184.html

Chapter 3   Teddy Joins Up

Teddy was educated at Eton before attending the Royal Military College Sandhurst. On 21 January 1893, he was commissioned as a 2nd Lieutenant in his local militia regiment, the 3rd Battalion Royal Sussex Regiment, of which his father was honorary Colonel and in which his older brother Bill was already commissioned. He was promoted to Lieutenant on 12 September 1894. On 7 December 1895, he transferred to the Seaforth Highlanders, his father's old regiment. Presumably, having decided to make the military his long-term career, he needed to transfer to a regiment "of the line", rather than the militia. Quite possibly it was always his intention to join the Seaforths, and he joined the Royal Sussex whilst waiting for a commission to become available: they were few and far between at a time of relative peace. Here, in fact, he had to take a demotion in rank and was gazetted 2nd Lieutenant. He was 21 years old.

It may seem strange that an Englishman from Sussex, a stone's throw from the English Channel, should join a Highland regiment named for Loch Seaforth in the Outer Hebrides, the very furthest north-west of Scotland. That decision was undoubtedly influenced by his father and his connections, and at the time of William Henry's joining the 72nd Regiment, as the Seaforths were then known, it was cheaper to buy a commission there than in more prestigious regiments such as the Guards. In January 1908, when writing to General

Granville Egerton, his former commanding officer in Crete, Teddy remarks on this fact when talking about his father's generation, who were then dying out:

"It's funny to think that in the Crimea nearly all the offices of the 72nd were Englishmen."[13]

Arguably, national identity within the Union was more fluid in those days of Empire.

Origins of the Seaforth Highlanders

The Seaforth Highlanders were founded in 1777 by Kenneth Mackenzie, the 1st Earl of Seaforth (second creation), the grandson of the rebellious 5th Earl (1st creation) who was attainted for his participation in the 1715 Jacobite rebellion. In order to show gratitude for being allowed to re-purchase the confiscated family estates from the Crown, Kenneth promised to raise a Regiment to serve the King. This was especially necessary at the time due to the American War of Independence which had started in 1775. The Regiment's name is derived from Loch Seaforth, or Loch Siophort in Gaelic, a sea loch which forms the dividing line between Lewis and Harris and then a Clan Mackenzie heartland.

Over the next hundred and twenty years, the Regiment saw much service, and the Battle Honours carried on the Regimental Colour include Carnatic, Hindoostan, Mysore, Cape of Good Hope 1806, Maida, Java and South Africa

---

[13] Egerton Archive - M.1994.112.32

1835. The Regiment had then been sent to Crimea, where Teddy's father had seen action at the Battle of Sevastopol, before travelling to India, as part of Colin Campbell's force to suppress the Indian Mutiny.

It is interesting to consider the role that Highland regiments such as the Seaforths played in rehabilitating the image of the Gael in the British national consciousness. It was only in 1746, a mere thirty years before their creation, that the largely Highland-raised army under Bonnie Prince Charlie had seriously threatened the Hanoverian grip on the Crown. The suppression that had followed was vicious, with the wearing of the kilt proscribed, as well as the disestablishment of the Chiefs through the abolition of heritable jurisdictions, and the banning of the carrying of weapons. The army, by contrast, allowed Gaels to continue to express their martial culture and represented an attractive career for many. In the latter decades of the 18th century, the Highland Regiments played a key role in rehabilitating the image of this part of the Kingdom. So much so, that King George IV was prepared to cloak himself in tartan and wear a kilt on his famous visit to Edinburgh in 1822, thereby laying the foundation for the 19th century love of all things Highland. It was noted by the Aldershot News in 1895 that nearly half of the Battalion spoke Gaelic, reflecting the strong Highland roots of the rank and file.[14]

By the time that Teddy joined in 1895, the Victorian passion for the romance of tartan was at its height and Regiments wore tartan that had no connection

---

[14] Recounted in Granville Egerton's Reminisces of a Seaforth Highlander Vol II, National War Museum M.1994.112.93

with the Gaels of the Highlands, including all of the Scottish Lowland regiments, which in 1881 were authorised to wear Black Watch tartan trews[15]. There is no doubt that their attire was taken very seriously and was a valued part of their identity. The uniform attracted a lot of attention wherever they went in the world, from the Cretan peasants to the German forces in the First World War, the kilts in particular made them stand out and created a strong sense of Esprit de Corps. The idea of wearing heavy woollen kilts and horsehair tasselled sporrans in roasting hot locations such as Sudan or Crete, may seem absurd to us today, but so they did. Nowhere in the diaries does Teddy refer to his clothing in a derogatory manner. In fact, in Crete Granville Egerton, describes them going into town after Sunday parade:

> *Afterwards, Messrs Egerton and Campion very handsomely dressed in serge uncovered helmets, kilts, steel scabbards and wearing all their decorations, good conduct badges and bravery awards, proceeded to the city where they promenaded on the Quay and were very much admired.*

This did change over time however, and by the Boer War the Highland regiments wore khaki aprons to cover their kilts and provide some camouflage. Kilts also had drawbacks in the tropical sun – especially sunburn of the exposed flesh on their legs. That said, the kilt cannot have been altogether impracticable or it would surely have been abandoned. Ironically, one can

---

[15] https://www.scottishmilitarydisasters.com/index.php/titles-sp-26803/26-smd/34-quick-guide-to-the-scottish-regiments

imagine that in the trenches of the First World War a woollen kilt might have been more desirable than cotton trousers, as its far warmer when wet, although its pleats provided ample hiding place for fleas and lice, and latterly the men would learn to their cost that poison gas burned uncovered body parts.

From the Frontline of History

Chapter 4 The Crete Crisis of 1897

Regrettably, we have no record of Teddy's days of training at Aldershot or his first 18 months of service in the Seaforth Highlanders. In one of his later letters to Egerton, he makes reference to an account he had written of those days, but it has either not survived or at least not been found. However, we do know that the 1st Battalion Seaforths had recently returned from service in Tipperary in 1894 and were now stationed in the Salamanca Barracks.

The first narrative available to us is a diary kept during Teddy' first overseas posting. He was initially sent to Malta on 26 January 1897, to be stationed in the St Elmo Barracks, considered to be the worst in Malta and known as the Bear Pit, before being sent to Crete on 16 March 1897. The posting to Crete was as part of a small detachment of Seaforth Highlanders that were participating in one of the international community's earliest peace keeping missions.

The Cretan conflict, largely forgotten in modern times, was a symptom of the long decline of the Ottoman Empire, during which insurgent Greek nationalists had sought to liberate Christian communities from their Ottoman rulers and join them to Greece. In Crete, this had led to inter-ethnic conflict as the Christian and Muslim communities vied with each other for the upper hand. In February 1897, there had been reports of significant massacres of Muslim communities, particularly around Canea, the capital, and the Sublime Porte's

From the Frontline of History

Ambassador to Britain had complained that some 2,000 Muslims had been massacred in nearby villages[16].

In response, the international community of the day, which is to say, Great Britain, Austria-Hungary, France, Germany, Italy and Russia, established the International Squadron, which committed to protecting the Muslim inhabitants of the island. Not only was this to save many lives in the local community, but it also provided the means of preventing all-out war breaking out between Greece and Turkey. In other words, it was a peacekeeping mission, and it had many characteristics that are very familiar to us today. One can certainly draw many parallels with the international community's response to the wars that broke out following the disintegration of Yugoslavia in the 1990s[17].

The International Squadron divided the island of Crete into areas of responsibility which were then portioned out between the participating nations, although Canea as the capital, was a shared responsibility and was defined as the International Zone.

---

[16] Mick McTiernan – A very bad place indeed for a soldier, the British involvement in the early stages of the European intervention in Crete 1897-8

[17] In the diary, Teddy's fellow officer - Lieutenant Daniell, speculates that this was how wars would be conducted in the future, with the international community stepping in to break up the fights between smaller nations. Granville Egerton, in a later note, questions this, pointing out that the international intervention in China[17] had not been going well. Perhaps they were both to some extent right.

From the Frontline of History

On 18 March 1897, the 1st Battalion Seaforth Highlanders, consisting of 18 officers and 582 other ranks, were ordered from their station in Malta to Crete. On 24 March 1897, D Company was landed at the port of Canea, in the International Zone, while the remainder of the Battalion were landed at Candia (modern-day Heraklion) which lay in the centre of the British zone. D Company was under the leadership of Captain Granville Egerton, with 2nd Lieutenants Daniell and Teddy Campion under him. On landing at Canea, the small group of three officers kept a diary between them.[18] They were subsequently joined by G Company on 6 April with Lieutenants Gaisford and Stockwell, and Major S.B. Jameson came to command both companies.[19]

Captain Egerton was an experienced officer. Having received his commission in 1879, he had served during the Second Afghan War, where he was seriously wounded in the Battle for Kandahar, when the British defeated the Afghan army under the command of Ayub Khan in 1880. Egerton recovered to pursue a long and distinguished military career. In 1882, he saw service during the Egyptian Campaign and fought at the Battle of Tel-el-Kebir. He later transferred from the Seaforth Highlanders to command the 1st Infantry Brigade in

---

[18] This was retained by Granville Egerton, their Commander and it can now be found among Egerton's papers at the National Army Museum. The diary is listed as being by Granville Egerton, but was in fact written in a number of different hands, each of the officers of D Company writing a section when the mood took them. Unquestionably, the greatest part of it was written by Teddy Campion, and it may well have been his idea in the first place.

[19] In a poignant footnote added in 1920, Egerton outlines the fate of these men, with Major Jameson retiring as Colonel having commanded the 2nd Seaforths, Egerton commanding the XIX Yorkshire Regiment and becoming a Major General in 1912 and retiring in 1919. Colonel Daniell, Colonel Gaisford, Major Campion and Major Stockwell all fell in the Great War.

From the Frontline of History

September 1909 and subsequently the 52nd Lowland Infantry Division in March 1914, which he led at Gallipoli. He retired with the rank of Major General in 1919 but went on to be appointed Colonel of the Highland Light Infantry between 1921-29. Remarkably, given his active service record, he lived on until 1951.

From the moment of their arrival, the Seaforths seem to have attracted a good deal of attention, no doubt on account of their idiosyncratic uniform. It seems hard to believe now, but the Seaforths conducted day-to-day duties dressed in their uniform of kilt and stockings – garb designed for the chilly inclement weather of the Highlands of Scotland and not the baking Mediterranean shores of Crete. They clearly made quite an impression on the other soldiers of the International Squadron who frequently came to visit their encampment (the ready availability of whisky may also have played a part in that). All the interactions seem to have been pretty good natured, at least between the forces of the International Squadron.

When sent to Crete, Teddy was 24 years old and just 16 months into his commission. He was the youngest of the officers and seemingly a bit of a joker. In the Battalion archive, there is a caricature of him at this time that has him dressed up as a baby with a cricket bat and baby's bottle in hand approaching the crease – perhaps as the "babe" of the regiment. He is regularly lambasted by his fellow officers for his cheek. The tone of the diary is certainly very light-hearted and good natured, and it seems that he was indulged by his senior officers with much affection, despite or even because of his irreverence.

Although Teddy had been serving in the regular army and the militia for the previous five years, this was his first experience of active service. As a subaltern he was responsible for supporting his commanding officer, Granville Egerton, noting his orders and ensuring they were followed. As we have seen, Egerton was a highly experienced officer who had seen much action and knew of the potential danger that surrounded them. By contrast, like many young men of his age, especially those that have yet to see the reality of war, Teddy manifests a braggadocio which would vanish in his later career. Perhaps this is unsurprising, given his upbringing in an upper class and traditionally military household at the height of Empire when pluck was lauded and cowardice despised. There is an extraordinary insouciance in Teddy's descriptions of the naval bombardments of insurgent positions in those early days – the impact and destructive force of those shells were being directed at others, to be sure, but the tenor of those opinions would change dramatically by the end of his career. It is almost as if the fighting between the Greek and Turkish forces were being observed from above, as though watching warring ants under a glass, rather than the real-life struggle that was playing out before them.

One gets the impression that although there was certainly very real danger on this mission, no one was greatly concerned about the prospect of being killed or injured. The naivety of this perspective would become all too clear the next year, when 15 British soldiers were killed and 35 wounded during the Candia riots on 6 September 1898. Teddy was in Sudan by then and commented morosely that the International Squadron should have taken the opportunity to nip the troubles in the bud when they had had the chance.

Whether by good management of the rebels or just good fortune, the Seaforths passed their time in Crete without any combat fatalities, although sickness was an issue. Typhoid – or enteric fever as it was then known – was a major problem and there were strict orders to drink only the boiled water and not the water for cooking and especially not any of the Cretan lemonade, which being made with local water was considered highly risky.

Their camp was outside Canea at the village of Halepa well away from the other troops and with *"the most glorious sea bathing"*[20] not fifteen yards from their tents. This led to some painful encounters with sea urchins, causing an issue for those unfortunate enough to stand on them and in turn prompting Egerton to ban sea bathing until a safer place could be found. The officers all got on very well and while their combat duties may have been relatively light, there was a lot of duty work, including relentless picquet duty. In the early days, the officers were on picquet duty for 12 hours at a time and many days in a row which was very wearing. Tongue firmly in his cheek, Teddy relates the excellent job he had done in guarding the seven flags of the Squadron through the night – hardly the work of heroes. The diary also includes the gentle ribbing of the romantic exploits of Daniell, who's amorous encounters with Indian ladies the subject of much speculation.

However, in the first week of April the atmosphere changed, and the detachment got its first taste of action when a large body of Bashi-Bazouks, the irregular Turkish forces, rushed towards the Akrotiri peninsular to confront the

---

[20] Egerton Archive - M.1994.112.98

From the Frontline of History

Christian forces based there. This precipitated a flurry of activity as the Seaforths were initially ordered to disarm the Bashi-Bazouks in Calicut, a nearby town that fell under Egerton's responsibility – presumably no easy task. Perhaps recognising the febrile atmosphere, the orders were later changed to allow the Bashi-Bazouks to retire. But the following day, once tempers had cooled, the Seaforths were once again sent to disarm these troops. They performed this task quite successfully, taking in nearly a hundred rifles with the promise of a thousand more.

As usual, Teddy's account is light-hearted and slightly flippant, but his entry is followed by a slightly sterner note from Egerton who states that it was in part due to their preparations that the situation did not get out of hand. Once can sense that the naïve, exuberant young officer on his first active duty is keen to show his mettle and be undaunted by the enemy and danger. His more experienced commanding officer, on the other hand, is keen to avoid any unnecessary confrontation with the warring parties.

After this tense situation, they were joined by G Company of the Seaforths on 7 April, and their group of officers now included Lieutenants Gaisford and Stockwell. Teddy's entries continue in a jovial and sardonic manner – recounting a march out under the Akrotiri heights that he went on with Gaisford and Egerton:

> *It was a real nice walk. We got clear of the stinks and smells of the town and the day reminded one of June in England – that most delightful*

time of year at home. What rot! Are we getting home sick? Not us! Thirsting for blood, which we can't get. I do feel so brave.

Much is then made of his being threatened with a beating with the birch and even court martial over the next days for his *"General cheek"*, *"Talking utter slush"* and *"writing abominable slush"*. Egerton writes that as this was his second trial, the tariff will be 168 strokes and *"well laid on"*!

Such gentle ribbing reflects the close knit nature of relationship between the officers of the Battalion, perhaps unsurprising as they often spent years or even decades in each other's company in often very tense situations. We imagine the Victorians as a dour bunch, but the collegiate banter in this diary makes clear that they were not so unlike us today.

Major Jameson arrived on 11 April to take over Command of the Seaforth Detachment, something that Egerton described as *"an awful smack in the eye"* for him and his leadership[21], given that everything had gone so well to that point. The next moment of excitement came on 15 April, when the Combined Admirals of the International Squadron decided to hold a Review of the international forces. This parade, which was quite an unusual event given the number of different nations present at the time in Crete, made a big impression, not only on the participants and the assembled media, but presumably on the local population too. It was clearly intended to send a

---

[21] Egerton Archive - M.1994.112.98

message to the warring parties demonstrating both the power and commitment of the international community.

The Seaforths made their own fun; being the first to line up on parade, they raised and maintained their flag in prime position for some time before the other nations scurried out to raise their own flags. Rear Admiral Harris, Britain's most senior naval officer present, was clearly impressed, stating: *"Our detachment of the Seaforth Highlanders made a most creditable appearance, and their smartness was much noted by the foreigners, including my colleagues."*[22]

Teddy was much amused by some of the colourful uniforms of the other powers – somewhat ironic given the Seaforths' own outlandish attire – and the sheer number of hangers on that came to inspect the parade proved more than a little wearing:

> *A never to be forgotten day. The great international review by the Combined Admirals, also by a mixed crowd of Maltese, mess visitors, cooks, vivandeurs, ladies and officers of all ranks and nations.....*
>
> *We were the first on the ground and our flag at the saluting point was for some time floating in sole grandeur until other nations not to be outdone sent furiously for their own. We saluted Amoretti as he wended down the line attended by Quirini and two fellows in the most*

---

[22] ADM116 Vol.2. Telegram No.476. Rear Admiral Harris to Admiral Sir John Hopkins 23 April 1897

marvellous costume – a conglomeration of all the colours of the rainbow – and a hideous combination it was. However, they thought themselves very smart.

The Combined Admirals kept us waiting a long time and when they at length arrived, they walked down the line and inspected us attended by a retinue that beggars all description. Has any regiment ever been inspected by such a crowd? Not only officers of every power, dressed in fancy carnival costume, but Ladies, Maltese cooks and mess waiters. Naval officers greeted one with a friendly nod as they passed, which needless to say, as we were at the "Present", we received with stony glares.

Egerton relates in the diary:

This international review was a sight that will probably never be seen again for 1,000 years.

However fine a sight the International Review might have been, it did not stop the march of history and on April 18 the Ottoman Empire declared war on Greece, triggering a heightened sense of nervousness in Crete. Consequently, the International Squadron sent a force made up of 75 British, 75 Austrians, 75 French, 90 Italians and two Italian guns to guard the neck of the Akrotiri Peninsula, just outside Canea, and to prevent the large body of insurgents camped there from breaking out, while also preventing any Bashi-Bazouks from breaking in and attacking them. Egerton was in command and Teddy went with him. Tensions were clearly running high, but Egerton managed to build a good rapport with the two warring parties and establish picquets in between their forces as Egerton writes[23]:

> *With these gentleman, Captain Egerton entered into excellent relations from the first and had frequent meetings with them under a flag of truce. At the beginning of the investment the neutrality was distinctly an armed one and the respective picquets and sentries were not above 500 yards distant from one another.*
>
> *Neither side trusted one another a yard. But as time went on, and the island quieted down, the neutral vigilance became easier. The worst danger was that the insurgents might get out of hand at one of their constantly recurring Saint's-day festivals and disobeying the orders of the Chiefs, who had really but little hold over them, make a rush to get through the outposts and attack the hated Turk in the valley beyond.*
>
> *Nothing serious ever happened, but for the two months that I was in command at Akrotiri, Campion and myself took it in turn every night to visit the sentries and patrol the neighbourhood after 12 midnight. I did not trust the Italians a yard and had no great confidence in the French, but my Austrian detachment officers and men were reliable to the last degree. The Italians were very fond of the English and were ready to black our boots and they have never forgotten how much we assisted*

---

[23] Egerton starts writing this in the third person before switching to first person.

towards a united Italy. The Austrians were on very friendly terms always, their officers were nearly all gentlemen, which was not certainly the case with most of the other foreign officers. The Russians we saw little of, they were mainly outside Canea on account of their rowdy habits. Their Colonel was an ex-Guardsman exiled from St Petersburg for his numerous enemies – he was often seen drunk.

The French were all Infanterie de la Marine, "Les Marsouines" riddled with Madagascar and Touguiu fever and undisciplined devils I thought. Captain Amoretti so often mentioned in this diary was an Italian Naval Officer in executive command of all the international troops, some 2,000 in number, at Canea. He was a delightful tactful man, who conducted his somewhat difficult task admirably.

During this period, the diary is essentially left until Teddy and Egerton returned, with their colleagues writing only two more entries before ceasing. After making a few more comments, none by Teddy, the diary was then finally abandoned and does not cover any of the period from June until 22 November 1897[24] when the Seaforths departed Crete for Malta on board the *S.S. Jelunga*.

---

[24] There is some confusion as to the exact date as Egerton states 22 November 1897 (M.1994.112.98), while 25 November is given by https://www.maltaramc.com/regmltgar/1seahldr.html

From the Frontline of History

In an account of the Crete Occupation written for the Green Howard's Gazette, Egerton gives a little more information on what he and Teddy got up to during those two months on the heights of Akrotiri[25]:

> *Foumis was, together with a certain Mr E. Venezelos, the leader or chief of the band of insurgent Cretans numbering some hundreds, with two or three guns, who occupied the peninsula of Akrotiri between Canea and Suda Bay....My duty with a cordon of 300 international troops was to hold the narrow neck of this peninsula and prevent the insurgents getting out to go for the Turks, or the Bashi Bazouks from Canea breaking in, in order to attack the Christian insurgents. Foumis and I used to meet frequently on the neutral ground between our respective outposts and as I said before we were always on the very best of terms. He had an awkward team to drive, as I well knew, and often assured me that he hoped if any of his men tried to break through the cordon that I would shoot them. I fancy they used to evade the sentries at night, but I am glad to say it never came to shooting anybody and my two months sojourn on the outposts passed off without any bloodshed or regrettable incident whatever.*

Egerton goes on to summarise his and Teddy's time in Crete:

> *We had shaves and excitements, rumours of attack by the insurgents, of outbreaks amongst the Turkish troops also on the island, marches*

---

[25] Egerton Archive - Some Reminiscences by Colonel Granville Egerton C.B. (written originally for The Green Howards' Gazette.) A 242.72.07 EGE

out to show the flag, outposts to protect the people gathering crops. Altogether the best summer's soldiering I ever did, or anyone ever did. The food was good, grapes glorious and game birds of sorts, and donkey loads of frozen snow came down daily from the mountains...the British contingent undoubtedly surpassed the others in every way; physique, drill clothing, equipment...

While no Seaforths were killed in action during this time, that did not mean that they went completely unscathed; 21 men of the British force died on service and four of them were Seaforths, two of whom died from enteric fever (typhoid) with the cause of the other two deaths unrecorded[26]. In the Sudan Campaign Diary there is a footnote reference to Teddy being ill for a week during the Cretan occupation and being nursed by Egerton, although there is no further detail.

After the Seaforths were sent to the Sudan, the International Occupation of Crete continued and much more intense fighting broke out during the Candia riots on 6 September 1898, when 15 British servicemen were killed and 35 wounded. On hearing this news in the depths of the Sudan on 14 September 1898, Teddy expressed his frustration:

---

[26] https://britishinterventionincrete.wordpress.com/category/european-intervention-crete/british-army-in-crete/

We heard at Dakhila of the fight in Crete – hang it: why didn't they let us at 'em when we were there – the job could have been much easier managed then than it will be now

Teddy's first overseas posting had been highly unusual for the time; close international cooperation and a peace keeping mission which has more in keeping with the late 20th century. He was young, naïve and keen to prove himself. But he was also diligent, hardworking and likable, making strong friendships, some of which would endure for the rest of his life. For a man brought up on the tales of his father, who had experienced the ferocious set-piece battles in Crimea and the Indian Mutiny, it must have seemed a bit of a let-down, but his next posting to Sudan would be very different.

From the Frontline of History

Teddy as a boy

East Sussex Brighton and Hove Record Office: DAN 4/3/2225

From the Frontline of History

Danny, Teddy's home, in the snow c.1905

The Great Hall, Danny c.1905

From the Frontline of History

William Henry Campion, Teddy's father, and his sisters Elsie and Joan

From the Frontline of History

Teddy as a newly commissioned officer in the Seaforth Highlanders 1895

(Highlanders Museum)

From the Frontline of History

The 'Babe of the Regiment', Teddy in 1896

(Highlanders Museum)

The Canea contingent of Seaforth Officers

From left: 2nd Lieut Stockwell, Capt Egerton, Maj. Jameson, 2nd Lieut Daniell, Surgeon Major Shine, 2nd Lieut Campion, Lieut Gaisford, Surgeon Captain Luther

(Highlanders Museum)

From the Frontline of History

With the rebels above Akrotiri. Teddy is directly in front of the rebel flag pole with Egerton on his left

From Egerton's album – captioned: My first visit to the insurgents, my white flag, Greek flag, 2nd Lieut Campion, Self, Surg Capt Baylor, Drummer Fairbairn, died of his wounds recd at the Atbara the following year

Image © National Museums Scotland

From the Frontline of History

Officers of 1st Battalion Seaforth Highlanders 1897, Teddy circled and below

(Highlanders Museum)

From the Frontline of History

Chapter 5   The Sudan Campaign

From the relative mundanity of the policing operation in Crete, Teddy's next posting would be much more arduous and a step into the unknown. If Crete was less familiar to Victorians than it might be to us today, it was at least still part of Europe and bound by the Mediterranean. The campaign against the Dervishes of the Sudan and their Khalifa would take Teddy deep into the heart of Africa into a place utterly different from the green hills and fertile fields of Sussex where he grew up.

Sudan had been a running sore for the British Empire ever since General Charles Gordon had been killed there in January 1885, at the end of a ten month siege, along with many of his Egyptian soldiers, when Khartoum had been captured by Muhammad Ahmad, the religious and political leader of the Dervishes, otherwise known as the Mahdi. The Mahdi did not outlive his rival for long, dying in June 1885, but the reins of the Mahdist state were taken up by the very able Abdullah Ibn-Mohammed Al-Khalifa.

These were the years of the "Scramble for Africa" and colonial powers were making inroads across the continent, creating spheres of influence and colonies. However, the Khalifa had his own expansionist plans and had invaded Ethiopia in 1887, sacking the capital of Gondar, and ultimately killing the Emperor Yohannes IV at the Battle of Metemma in 1889. He also invaded Egypt, which was nominally a British "protectorate"; and although he had been repulsed, there were concerns that with access to the Red Sea he could threaten the Suez Canal and Britain's crucial link to India. Doubtless, the British also did not want to leave a vacuum that could be filled by a rival nation. Dervish rule was not without cost, and Slatin Pasha, the Anglo-Austrian soldier and administrator, who had a deep knowledge of Sudan, estimated that some 75% of the normal population of Sudan had perished under its influence.[27] The decision was therefore taken, in conjunction with the Egyptians, to send a new expeditionary force under General Herbert Kitchener, who was appointed Sirdar or Commander, to assert Anglo-Egyptian hegemony over Sudan.

In support of this, on 5 Jan 1898, the 1st Battalion Seaforth Highlanders were ordered to leave the Lower St Elmo Barracks in Malta and embark for Egypt, where they arrived on 10 January 1898. They then made their way to the Kasr El-Nil Barracks in Cairo where they waited for orders to mobilise. These finally came on 27 February 1898 when the tortuous journey up the Nile to confront the enemy began. In Teddy's diary entry, the excitement is palpable.

A long and winding road

The distance from Cairo to Khartoum is 1,350 miles as the vulture flies, and it was a prodigious logistical challenge to move an army of sufficient scale across such a distance. It is true that the River Nile was used as a highway, but there were frequent obstacles and cataracts that had to be bypassed, which ultimately meant that it was necessary to use a variety of boat, train, and even

---

[27] Egerton Archive - M1994 112.83

camel, in conjunction with good old-fashioned marching, in order to move the Anglo Egyptian army into position to confront the Khalifa.

The first stop was Aswan (Assouan in Victorian times), where Teddy had a jolly time with a coterie of ladies who were either based there or who had followed the Battalion south. In particular, he recounts dining with the Misses Fraser, and laments having to leave such attractive company behind. There were also the temples of Philae and other sights of Ancient Egypt to be admired along the way, although he makes it clear that hieroglyphics were beyond him.

There is no doubt that the journey onward from Aswan was much more arduous. The regiment decamped into barges, which were lashed to steamboats for the journey upriver. This was a slow process and occasional unscheduled stops had to be made due to grounding on sandbanks or men falling overboard. The heat was also rising the further South they went, with the temperature at that time of year in the mid-high 30s Celsius. The officers at least had berths on board the steamboat *Amara*, but it seems likely the men were a good deal less comfortable. All were in the same boat, literally and metaphorically, on the next stage as they were transferred into Nuggers, a type of Nile sailing barge that was very uncomfortable, especially when so crammed with men.

They finally arrived at Darmali on 17 March, two and a half weeks after leaving Cairo. Darmali would be their base for much of their time in Sudan. Located close to the junction of the Atbara River and the Nile, it was well placed to divide the Khalifa's forces, with one army under his general Emir Mahmoud roaming the Atbara River and the remaining body of his forces at Khartoum. Mahmoud was the first target.

The Battle of Atbara

After their arrival at Darmali they swiftly marched along the Nile to Kunur, closer to the junction with the Atbara. Now that they were in Dervish country serious precautions were taken with the erection of a zariba, a thorn barrier typically used in Sudan, to protect the camp perimeter every night. General Gatacre, of whom Teddy had a very low opinion, also demanded onerous picquet duties of the men, and moreover made them sleep in all their gear and belts, which was very uncomfortable and much derided by Teddy as being unnecessary. It was at this time that the Seaforths had their first encounter with Dervish cavalry.

As Mahmoud retreated down the Atbara in the face of the allied forces, Kitchener pursued him, wanting to bring him to battle. The next three weeks were spent in an exhausting game of cat and mouse, with rumours of Mahmoud's shifting position driving Gatacre to test his men's patience with endless marches and long nights on watch. However, Mahmoud was running out of food for his army and was aware that if he didn't engage with the enemy soon, he might no longer have an army left for the fighting.

Mahmoud realised he would have to stand and fight and, bearing in mind the success of Dervish forces against a range of enemies in the past, including the British, he may well have thought that he had a good chance. He had numerical superiority on his side, with 15,000 troops to the 10,000-strong Anglo Egyptian force[28]. The Dervish also had 5,000 mounted Baggara horsemen against Kitchener's 500 cavalry. However, there can be little doubt as to which army had the more modern equipment, with the Anglo Egyptian forces able to deploy artillery, rockets and Maxim guns.

Thus it was that at 1 a.m. on 8 April, Teddy and his fellow troops marched towards Mahmoud's camp at Mutrus, arriving shortly before 6 a.m. Shortly thereafter the Anglo Egyptian artillery and machine gunners opened up a tremendous bombardment of the enemy's positions. For the next hour and twenty minutes, shells poured down onto the Dervishes with the fire so hot that Teddy writes:

> *I never dreamt for a moment they could stick this tremendous bombardment and when we rose up and moved off on the left opposite our point of attack I did so without feeling a tremor of nervousness, so absolutely certain did I feel that we should not see a single Dervish inside the zariba.*[29]

In this he was mistaken, as he would soon discover. The Dervishes had learned from their previous engagements with European forces and had dug themselves into trenches and foxholes which protected them from the artillery fire. As the British forces began to advance they started to feel the Dervish fire.

---

[28] https://www.britishbattles.com/war-in-egypt-and-sudan/battle-of-atbara/
[29] This sentiment was echoed in the margin by Granville Egerton at a later date.

From the Frontline of History

As the Seaforths were placed directly behind the Cameron Highlanders, they had to be patient as they advanced despite the flying bullets. Teddy was now truly bloodied in combat, his first pitched battle, and one can read the tone of his writing changing:

> *The enemy now began to make their presence known and I began to know what the sound of a bullet was like. We advanced slowly over some 600 yards. At about 150 yards from the zariba, the enemy's fire really began to get hot and uncomfortably close, and one began to realise that it was not going to be such a soft thing.*
>
> *At about 20 yards from the zariba, the Camerons halted, knelt down, and poured a tremendous fire on the enemy's trenches. Still the beggars stuck to it[30].*
>
> *This halt was the most trying. Men in front commenced to fall; the first man I saw hit just in front of the Company had the top of his head blown off, the second fell hit in the legs. All this time we were doing nothing except waiting and hoping to goodness the Camerons would soon go on.*
>
> *Then we advanced and in a minute or two the zariba was torn away and we were through and the enemy were bolting. From this moment on all was as much confusion as hitherto had been all parade*

---

[30] Egerton relates that Mahmoud said that he did not care twopence for the artillery bombardment, but that the infantry fire was "Tal Shaitan" – the very devil. Egerton Archive - M.1994.112.93

steadiness. Our men and the Camerons all jumbled up. One had to do one's best to get hold of a dozen men and lead them on. All the trenches had to be cleared on the way, as the enemy occupied them and the pits, and even when badly wounded kept firing.

The men did not give them much chance; both wounded and dead in most cases got a bayonet shoved through them. And lucky it was so, since some waited till one had passed, lying doggo meanwhile, and then had a plug.

We advanced without any check right on the river, where we blazed away at the enemy escaping over some 500 yards of dry sand bed. The men began to calm down and look through their sights. The shooting was pretty good and most of the fugitives got dropped. Soon after, the cease fire sounded and in a moment or two the deafening roar of musketry ceased, giving place to a deafening roar of talking.

The hand-to-hand fighting had been fierce, but once the Dervishes had been forced from their trenches and protective foxholes, they suffered from the marksmanship of their pursuers. The battle was over by 08.30 a.m. with Mahmoud captured and his army put to flight.

The Dervish death toll was sobering and an omen of what was to come at Omdurman, with over 2,000 Dervish dead found inside the zariba and a large number of prisoners taken. By contrast, Kitchener's entire army had lost 80 killed and 479 wounded, with the Seaforths having six killed, including one officer, and 27 wounded. Some of Teddy's fellow officers were wounded, with both Vandeleur and MacLachlan having been shot. For a time, Teddy was concerned about Vandeleur's prospects, but once the bullet had been extracted from his wound he improved. Some had had a narrow escape as Teddy describes:

> *Corporal Lawrie has seven bullet holes in his kilt & clothes but is only just touched on the chest. The Pipe Major got a skiff on the neck, the Sergeant Major a spear through his kilt.*

Looking at the casualty list does not tell the whole story; this was a bloody and fierce battle and the soldiers present remembered it as such. Granville Egerton wrote in his reminisces that he had no doubt that half of the very severe casualties were due to their own fire, and he notes that as there was little over half an hour of actual hand-to-hand fighting it was actually a very costly battle.[31]

Nonetheless, the battle had been won and the enemy's General captured. The army now had to rest and regroup before marching on Khartoum. After several days of very gruelling marches, the Seaforths arrived back in Darmali where they were to spend much of the next months.

The time was spent largely in fatigues that were literally make-work schemes to keep the men occupied and prevent boredom setting in. There was a good

---

[31] By contrast, Egerton compares this to the casualty rate at the battle of the Modder River during the Boer War which lasted all day and had casualties of 483. Egerton Archive - M.1994.112.93

deal of illness too, with the dreaded enteric fever never far away. At one point in May, 60 men were invalided back to Cairo, a significant proportion of the battalion's manpower.

Teddy colourfully describes the passage of a day in his diary:

> *Get up, hastily swallow a cup of cocoa, light a cigarette and find 50 bearded looking ruffians at the quarter guard. We get tools and commence to fill up a huge hole - why, no one quite knows, or cares – but you must not leave the men alone and on no account are they to be allowed to wash. So you keep them at it till time for breakfast – one goes back for a bath – breakfast porridge and a lump of heart – (sometimes varied with a weird and wonderful looking kidney – but usually we have a fair breakfast). Then orderly room. Return at about 10 a.m. Work for the day finished. Everything is getting hot. Order ginger ale – drink it, have another. It all comes out and trickles down your forehead. Go to your house?? Or dog–hole – gasp – look at thermometer: 104 degrees. Have another ginger ale on strength of it. Write diary, begin letter, hand all wet from perspiration smudges it. Lie down – perspire fearfully – swear at the flies. Try and kill one, very exhausting – have another ginger ale. 12 O'clock go to sleep – wake up 1 p.m. Lunch – everyone rather slack – read paper – long for 4 p.m. Have a small gin and ginger ale – tea. It begins to get cooler. Get a rifle, trudge off into the desert and shoot at a gazelle – this is great fun.*

Return 6 p.m. very hot and thirsty. Have a small gin and Bradford[32]. Visitors come round. Everyone bucks and talks; this is a most enjoyable time of day. Change for dinner – have an excellent dinner – everyone cheery and fit. Drink a bottle of Pilsner and begin to feel life is worth living – go to bed 10 p.m.

There were frequent brigade marches into the desert where the men were made to shoot at targets – mostly bushes or trees – in order to keep their eye in. However, there was also time for some pleasure, especially when a delivery of 6,000 shotgun shells arrived, of which Teddy snaffled 600. Most evenings he would ride out into the desert and shoot sandgrouse or doves to supplement the company's stores.

Teddy was also heavily involved in organising the regular Gymkhanas that were held, as much intended to keep the men occupied and diverted as entertained. These included a range of races and competitions between the different regiments, including a camel race for the officers and donkey race for the NCOs and men, which must have been comical, as well as more traditional horse racing in which Teddy is a frequent and successful competitor. There was a healthy dose of inter-regimental rivalry. All of this helped pass the time while the Expedition force waited for orders to march on Khartoum.

In conjunction with his fellow old Etonians, he even found time to send a telegram to Eton College on the Fourth of June, when the school celebrates

---

[32] Gin & Bradford – another name for a Martini

the birthday of George III, one of its major patrons, saying: *"Etonians British Brigade, Sudan, drink Floreat Etona ex fluvis Nile"*.

Unlike some of his fellow officers, such as Egerton, he didn't take any leave during this period, possibly in part due to the expense. When Egerton returns from a month's leave on 6 June, he said that it cost him £85 – equivalent of nearly £12,000 today[33] This was well beyond Teddy's means.

Unsurprisingly, Teddy did get very disillusioned with the endless waiting and pointless fatigues and didn't waste the opportunity to say so in his diary. Kitchener may have been waiting until he had all the necessary logistics in order, especially the railway, before making his final push on the Dervish capital; but for the men it was hot and dull and no amount of regimental games or concerts was going to change that.

Teddy took time to reflect on the media coverage of the Battle of Atbara, and this is a theme that he will return to later in his diaries with growing frustration – particularly during the First World War:

> *The mail came in last night. There were some more letters about the Battle of the Atbara – really we have I think had quite enough "slush" written by now. The D.T. was bad enough in all conscience – but some other effusions have been worse. I think it is now time the papers closed*

---

[33] https://www.in2013dollars.com/uk/inflation/1898?amount=85

From the Frontline of History

> *correspondence on this affair, which though no doubt a brilliant victory has been gushed over to – I think – too large an extent.*

For most of July the diary is put aside, not just because Teddy was "fed up", but also because he had run out of paper until Egerton brought him a new notebook on his return from leave in Cairo. In August once can sense that the wheels of the campaign are grinding back into motion. The wounded are returning from hospital, the railway arrives in Darmali, and other regiments start to arrive from down river in anticipation of what is to come.

One piece of good news for Teddy was that he was promoted to Lieutenant on 4 August, a promotion which he felt was overdue and, after the year he had had in Crete and Sudan, who can blame him.

Teddy also somehow acquired a camera, and starts for the first time to include some photos in the diary. Sadly, many of these have faded with time, but a few can still be made out.

On 14 August, the army was finally deploying for the march on Khartoum and Teddy was able to say farewell to Darmali; no tears were shed on that score. However, with the army on the move, some of the more excessively rigorous and paranoid aspects of General Gatacre's leadership once again came to the fore, with Teddy very critical of his orders, writing on 18 August:

> *Played at soldiers last night – it is a very good game. You take out your regiment all dressed up in marching order and you crowd them up as close as possible. Then you allow most of them to take off their*

accoutrements – but some are compelled to sleep fully belted up. Two sentries from each company are posted and told to keep a very sharp look out, as Dervishes may attack at any moment. Privately, you inform your sentries not to get too excited as there are no Dervishes within 50 miles[34] and you also tell them they are on not account to fire without orders from their company officer.

Then you lie down and try to sleep, but at frequent intervals you go round your sentries and again caution them not to fire or get excited. At length, after a weary night, comes the first faint blush of dawn streaking across the morning sky, but just before this you are awoken by a terrific blazoning of bugles, the rolling of drums, the skirl of pipes. This is, I believe, to give the enemy a chance of knowing where you are, or else as a warning to him that you are ready to attack. This the finale of the night's farce – and with the knowledge, that, if the enemy knew, how he would laugh, you sip your tea.

We are living in stirring times – a corporal of the company has just come up and whispered excitedly in my left lug that, if the alarm goes, the Company will immediately – whatever happens – take off their trews and don the kilt. After which, when fully accoutred, they will fall in on the zariba in order to repel the attack – for which the alarm was sounded. The above needs no comment, for crass idiocy and inane lunacy, it really takes the bun–buttered. And we are 50 miles from the

---

[34] In the margin – N.B. which is <u>fact</u>

enemy and the cavalry have only been in an hour, having reported that fact?!!

And again, on 19 August:

It really is ridiculous. Here are we, as four fine regiments as there are in the British army, all sitting staring over the zariba during the night, sleeping fully accoutred, sentries with fixed bayonets, officers on patrol, and we know there is just about as much chance of an attack as there is of an iced whiskey & soda. Do the Egyptian army with all their experience do this? They're not such fools. The consequence of all this tommy rot is that the men get nervous and excited, they never get their proper sleep and doing hard work during the day, they must deteriorate. But what sickens one is that there is no need for it – absolutely no need whatever.

As August went on, they moved nearer to the enemy and were joined by other regiments including the Guards, the Lancashire Fusiliers and the Northumberland Fusiliers. The army was now gaining its final shape for the showdown with the Khalifa. They marched past The Gate of Shabluka[35], the entrance to the Shabluka Gorge where the Nile passes through a narrow canyon, but they met no opposition. The marches were long and hot, with many soldiers falling out along the way, especially those less well acclimatised to the heat.

---

[35] Modern day Sabaloka

From the Frontline of History

On 1 September they were outside Omdurman, Khartoum's near neighbour, and heard reports of a large Dervish force coming out to meet them. After so many months of waiting, Teddy's excitement is palpable:

> *By 2.30 p.m. the whole army was formed up to receive what we were told was going to be the Dervish attack. It was a very fine sight – the whole British Division in line with the black regiments away on our right. In front, a dead level plain – level as a billiard table - and we were asked to believe that the Dervishes were going to attack over this ground – Whew! If they had! But it was an impossibility – no force could have lived under the British fire on this utterly flat front for 5 minutes. However, we laid down and hoped, but of course in vain and as I write now at 6 p.m. we are still waiting, but not expecting. Yet it may be possible that he will attack us tonight but I think far from likely. Our zariba is made and if the tremendous precautions we take were of any good, we are certainly ready for him. If he don't attack tonight, we are certain to go on tomorrow when I pray god, we may meet him in the open, have a good fight and utterly thrash him & enter Khartoum before the evening.*

> *We hear the force in front of us is very strong – estimated at 20,000 men & the Khalifa's flag has been seen with them. Everything points to a good fight tomorrow. All I hope is we catch him in the open.*

Even at this early stage, Teddy's analysis of what was to become the battlefield was entirely correct. The flat plain offered the Anglo-Egyptian forces a tremendous field of fire, which would test any opposing army severely. One can only imagine that the Khalifa and his generals felt that the plain also afforded their cavalry some advantage, but as we shall see that proved unfounded.

The Battle of Omdurman

We now turn to Teddy's eyewitness account of the Battle of Omdurman:

> *Stood to our arms 3.30 a.m., nothing occurred. At 5 a.m. the cavalry went out and sent back word that the enemy were advancing. It seemed almost too good to be true – but one saw the cavalry still out on both flanks of the hill on our left and they still sent back word that the enemy were advancing – soon the cavalry retired and we waited. The men were ordered to sit down, so as not to show our strength.*
>
> *And then, all of a sudden, we saw their banners in the distance and knew they were really coming – coming to the slaughter, for it could be nothing less, over this level plain. No finer field of fire could be imagined. They came on in one long line; then the centre held back and both right and left flanks swung round. That on their left flank looked the strongest, but there were tremendous numbers advancing in our centre with a great many banners.*

From the Frontline of History

At about 2,000 yards range our artillery opened fire – straight at his centre – short at first – but the range was soon obtained and shell were plumped bang into the midst of the Khalifa's ranks.

I suppose no-one in the Anglo-Egyptian army will ever again behold such a magnificent sight as this advance of the Dervishes. On they came, long white lines – line behind line – banners waving and making a curious cheering noise, or hardly cheering – more of a cackling nature. Never, I suppose, will any of us again see such a grand display of fanatical bravery, such an utter disregard of death. It was a magnificent spectacle. Here and there one could see their Emirs boldly riding far in front to, by their own dauntless courage, inspire the same in their men

Shells were bursting all among them, but they didn't seem to mind a bit and came sweeping on – a grand finale to Mahdiism.

At 1,500 yards we opened fire – steady section volleys – the Maxims joining in. His whole front was swept with what must have been a terrific fire, but they still came on. Each officer was directing volleys on conspicuous points. Suddenly, at about 1,100 yards, the cavalry attempted a charge but were almost immediately bowled over. At 1,000 yards, they were fairly checked and retired.

The attack on our right flank seemed to fare somewhat better and they got to within some 500 yards. But nearer no force in the world could have got in the face of the devilish fire poured in on them.

So far, we had had very few casualties. Bullets were occasionally knocking about spitting up the dust here & there & sometimes coming pretty close, but now, all of a sudden, they seemed to come closer.

Stretcher bearers were seen, doubling up, and told the effect: two men in my company and two men in the company on my right were all down within a few minutes.

One discovered that a lot of the enemy's riflemen had occupied a slight dip in the ground about 1,000 yards distant and were firing at us. We fired for some 10 minutes to a quarter of an hour varying our range from 700 – 1,000 yards, but failed to dislodge them. They were in such a position that it required the ground behind the lip of the dip to be well searched by Shrapnel. Accordingly, an Egyptian battery was sent for and after five or 10 more minutes of rifle and Shrapnel fire they got up and bolted.

The attack on our right front was now retiring, heavily shelled by the gunboats & so far the fight was finished. The enemy were shelled for some time retiring and then the whistle sounded. Everyone ceased fire and the cavalry went out. The whole force now moved out of the zariba and marched on Omdurman.

From the Frontline of History

As we approached the shoulder of the hill, firing suddenly began on our right. The top of the hill was also held by some 4 or 500 Dervishes. Firing on our right and right rear became heavier. A Sudanese battalion opened out and advanced on the hill. We now began to realise something was up and in another moment knew the enemy were strongly attacking our right & right rear.

The 1st Brigade swung right round and advanced towards the right of the hill. The 2nd Brigade went on to the left to threaten the enemy's retreat. The Sudanese assaulted the hill in grand style, an officer on a white horse rode in leading his men right up to the top — a fine performance. We now came in view of what was going on: MacDonald's Brigade were in a square and were being hard pressed, the enemy charging close up. On the left of his square was a large gap some 400 yards in length. The Egyptian companies were forming to fill it up, but it took a long time and while it was being done the gap formed a grand opportunity to the enemy. Their cavalry made a charge on the left corner of the square and got to within 15 yards. We now thought that the Camerons and half of ourselves would advance and fill up the gap but instead, worse luck, we were forced to the right some 100 yards — halted & pivoted — and the gap was now filled up. Volley after volley were fired at the enemy. The native regiments behaved splendidly and had they not stood steady things would have been very serious as the British Brigade would have had to form square and we should probably have been fired into by the Sudanese.

From the Frontline of History

Enormous numbers of the enemy now fled across our front, but the Egyptian and Sudanese fire very badly and killed very few – the only time they are any good with the rifle is shooting at men five yards off from the hip and even then they often miss and are very dangerous. Firing was now stopped and the Egyptian cavalry charged down from our right. The fight was finished, the Khalifa's army smashed & scattered and one of the prettiest battles ever fought was at an end.

We formed up and marched off on Omdurman & we heard of the disastrous charge of the 21st Lancers – while reconnoitring behind and south of the left hand hill, they appear to have suddenly come under a heavy fire emanating, as they imagined, from 2 or 300 Dervish spearmen. They were too close to do anything but go on and over bad and heavy ground and had to cut their way through. It was without doubt a charge worthy of British arms, carried out with all that dash and bravery that have before now distinguished our cavalry regiments. At the same time it was reckless & blind, the ground was unknown and evidently had not been reconnoitred, which from the Cavalry Drill book I always imagined was the duty of the ground scouts. While not wishing in any way to disparage the gallant 21st, and fully recognising the brilliant dash and impetuosity of their charge, I cannot but think that there must be faulty tactics when cavalry blindly hurl themselves over unknown ground against unknown numbers of the enemy. Their loss in this charge was 70 killed & wounded - the killed hacked up past recognition.

We halted for an hour outside Omdurman and from a small creek drank the filthiest water I have ever tasted. We then marched on into Omdurman and bivouacked outside the big wall. The stench was awful and the utterly filthy unsanitary state of the town is past all description.

Losses are as follows: Seaforths 18, Camerons 21, two officers, Lincolns 18, Warwicks 14, one officer killed. In all, on our own side, about 500 killed & wounded. Hopkinson wounded; Caldecott of the Warwicks killed; Frankie Rhodes wounded; Colonel Sleggett wounded; Measham wounded; Bobby Grenfell killed; and Howard (Times correspondent) killed. Howard was killed by a shell fired either by the enemy, or by gunboats, or the 32nd Field Battery – no one knows quite which - while he was with the Sirdar inside Omdurman near the Khalifa's house.

The enemy's killed have been carefully counted by officers and amount to about 7,000 – quite double this number must I think have been wounded. A great many were found in front of the 1st Brigade, a testimony to the excellent long-range practise we must have made.

The enemy's force must have numbered about 40,000 – Neufeld says about 60,000 left Omdurman the night before the fight and that about 20,000 deserted during the night.

This fight has shown what a nonsensical thing a zariba is in the daytime with British troops behind it. It gave the enemy a huge mark to fire at and it compelled us to fire standing up. Had we in the morning before the fight dragged the zariba away in rear, a work of a few moments, and had just lain down, our fire must have been far more effective & we must have had fewer casualties. To expect men to continue firing at 1,400 – 1,000 yards for an hour with fixed bayonets in a standing position is of course absurd. Of course we did do great execution, as has been shown by inspecting the dead on the field of battle, but we must have done far more in a lying down position

The surprise in the 2nd fight of the enemy's attack is curious; how the Sirdar did not have information that he was forming again I cannot make out. Either the gunboats or the cavalry or his own glasses should have seen them. As it was, I think there is little doubt the Sirdar was over confident, sure that they were thrashed & naturally very keen to head them from Omdurman, but it very nearly turned out a bad business. We have to thank the native regiments for standing as they did, had they not, though I do not for a moment doubt the issue would have been the same, the casualties would have been numerous & probably a fight more of the nature of Abu Klea would have occurred.

And so, one of the last great battles of the nineteenth century came to an end. The bravery and dash of the Dervish forces were no match for the Maxim gun, not to mention the steady and controlled fire from well-trained troops – especially over that plain, flat as a billiard table. Egerton recounts that his company fired 60 volleys into the enemy at Omdurman, a ferocious rate of fire from standing infantry.[36] Why had the Khalifa chosen to fight the battle in such a way? Why hadn't he dug into Omdurman or made defences similar to Mahmoud's at Atbara? In the manuscript of Egerton's memoires, annotated by General Sir Francis Reginald Wingate, who went on to command and administer in Sudan, it is stated that Slatin Pasha, the Allied Commander with long experience in Sudan, had heard that the Khalifa was going to attack during the night. In a cunning act of subterfuge, Pasha released captured Sudanese troops to tell the Khalifa that the British were themselves going to attack during the night. This apparently made the Khalifa change his plans at the last moment and fatefully fight during the day.[37]

But the Anglo-Egyptian force had not had it all its own way, and it is interesting to note Teddy's critical comments on Kitchener's complacency. Teddy also felt that without the resolve of the Egyptian and Sudanese regiments the situation could have deteriorated, and the allied casualties would have been a lot higher.

As Teddy would later find, his future wars would technologically be more closely matched, and his opponents would largely eschew set piece battles. One lesson that might have been learned better from Omdurman was that infantry advancing towards machine guns are unlikely to come off well; a lesson to be learned over and over during the First World War.

The army stayed at Khartoum for a surprisingly short time. Presumably the supply lines were stretched and there was no need for them to stay with the

---

[36] Egerton Archive – M1994.112.98
[37] Egerton Archive – M1994.112.97

From the Frontline of History

Dervish force so utterly destroyed. There was a little sightseeing and Teddy gathered some mementoes, including one of Gordon's roundshot which he wanted to make into a paperweight. While Teddy missed out on attending the memorial service to Gordon that was held in Khartoum, he did get the opportunity to visit Omdurman and the Mahdi's tomb, which was still standing, although damaged by shell fire. He did not think much of it:

> *Marched into Omdurman. I never want to go inside the beastly place again – dead donkeys – dead horses and a dead man or two laid about everywhere. I was nearly sick and on returning to camp several of the men were.*

> *The Mahdi's tomb struck one as being a regularly jerry built thing – thin walls – in fact I was not impressed by it. The howitzers had knocked enormous holes in it, but the walls were too thin for them to really make much effect.*

By 6 September, only four days after the battle, troops were being shipped back down river to Dakhila at the confluence of the Nile and Atbara rivers. On 8 September, the Seaforths disembarked to begin their slow passage downstream. Conditions were tough, and in a letter written to his mother, Teddy complains:

> *At the moment I am in a small sailing gyassa with 75 men in her! Simply packed like sardines, hardly sitting room, much less lying down. We have had two of what I think have been quite the worst days I have*

> spent in the Sudan. A blazing sun, a boat chock full of men, no breeze to help us, and floating down at about four or five miles an hour. It is awful work, but we are going in the right direction & the men say it's all downhill – so we are happy.

As they clocked up the miles, more and more food became available and after so long on miserable rations they were eagerly consumed by Teddy:

> I bought up bread, Rosbach beer & other luxuries – very expensive – but do we not deserve it? A fizzy drink & a loaf of bread, it don't sound so very extraordinary, but to us, who have been gnawing hard biscuit & drinking Nile water it is bliss. ….
>
> ….Got some provisions – chickens! Whew! What a 'sock' I'm going to have….
>
> …Got some eggs! & [ate] 'em for breakfast – 2 each – ripping.
>
> …What a greedy pig I am – got some spuds – spuds & chickens for lunch – it is glorious.

He finally arrived in Luxor on 16 September, ten days after leaving Omdurman, from whence he could take the train to Cairo. There the Seaforths stayed in the Citadel rather than the Kasr El-Nil Barracks, a fact bemoaned by Teddy as it added to the expense and money was always tight. As civilisation and all its comforts allowed him to unwind after a gruelling six months, he could reflect on his experiences, particularly that of the battle. Writing to his mother he says:

> *Whenever I think of the fight I think how wonderfully lucky we have been. Had the Khalifa only held onto Omdurman, dug trenches & holes like at Atbara – we should have taken a week to turn him out. For they fought as they have never fought since Abu Klea, with desperate fanatical bravery, and had they done this inside Omdurman the casualties would have been very enormous. But they must have been very confident, they came as if they were certain of smashing us. Their force has been estimated at between 40 & 50,000 men – their killed have been counted and amount to 7,000 odd. A great many dead were found in front of the British Division, which shows our firing was good. Poor beggars, I am, in a way, sorry for them.*

A bitter pill for Teddy to swallow was that despite having served in two active-service overseas postings, and not having had a long summer leave for two years, he would be denied Christmas at home.

> *We are being treated very badly; we, who have had no leave whatever for nearly two years, and have missed two summer leaves, have been placed in exactly the same category as those who had a good leave from Crete. It is, I think, a great shame. After all this time, I did expect a real good long leave - 3½ months at least - but what annoys me most is that I shall not be at home for Christmas – the one time of year that I would soonest be with the family.*

Such was the soldier's lot.

Loading up with fuel when going up the Nile

Nuggers on the Nile from the Daily Graphic

From the Frontline of History

Teddy and Egerton outside their tent, Image © National Museums Scotland

Teddy by the Nile, taken by Egerton, Image © National Museums Scotland

Seaforths storming the zariba at Atbara from the Daily Graphic

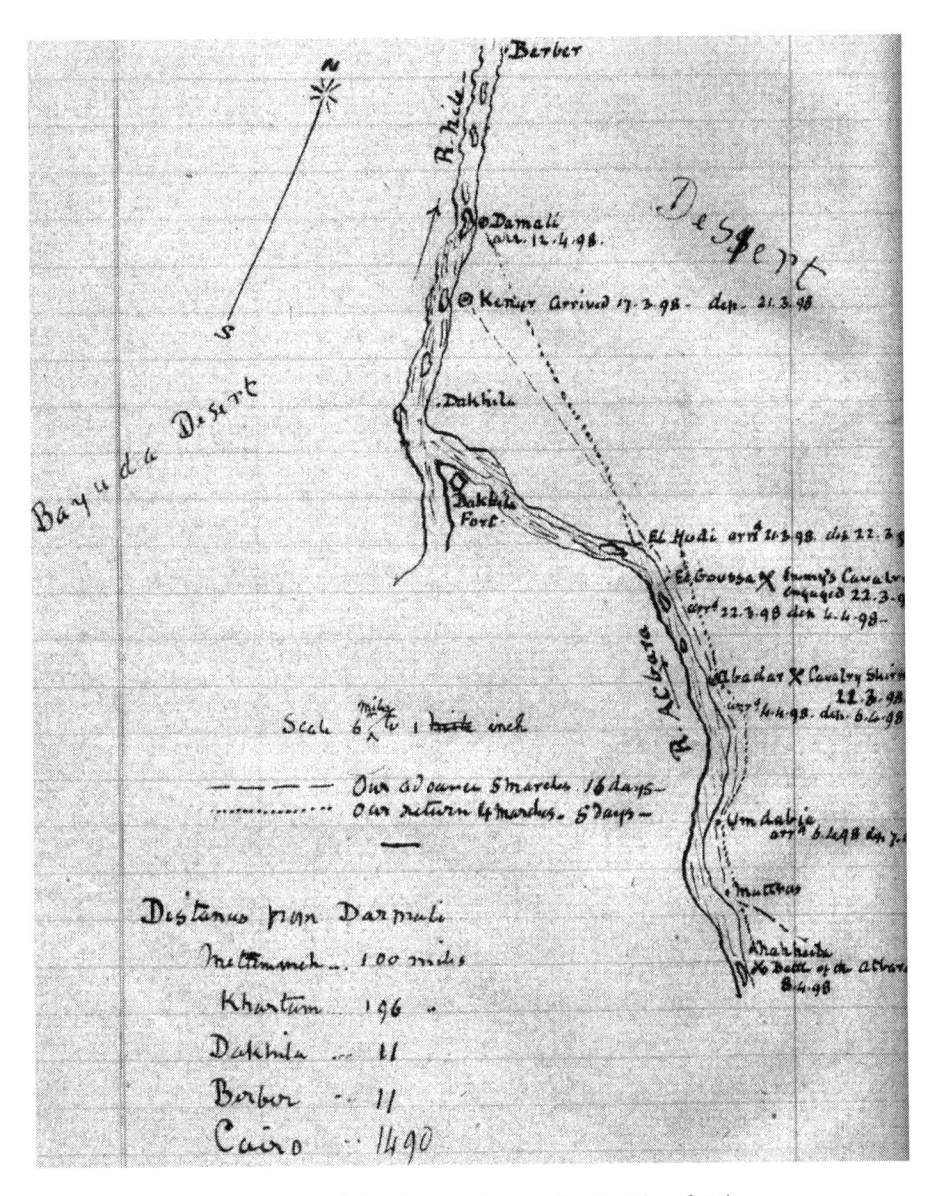

Teddy's map of the Campaign to the Battle of Atbara

From the Frontline of History

Waking up before the Battle of Omdurman

The last sight of Darmali as the Seaforths head home down the Nile

From the Frontline of History

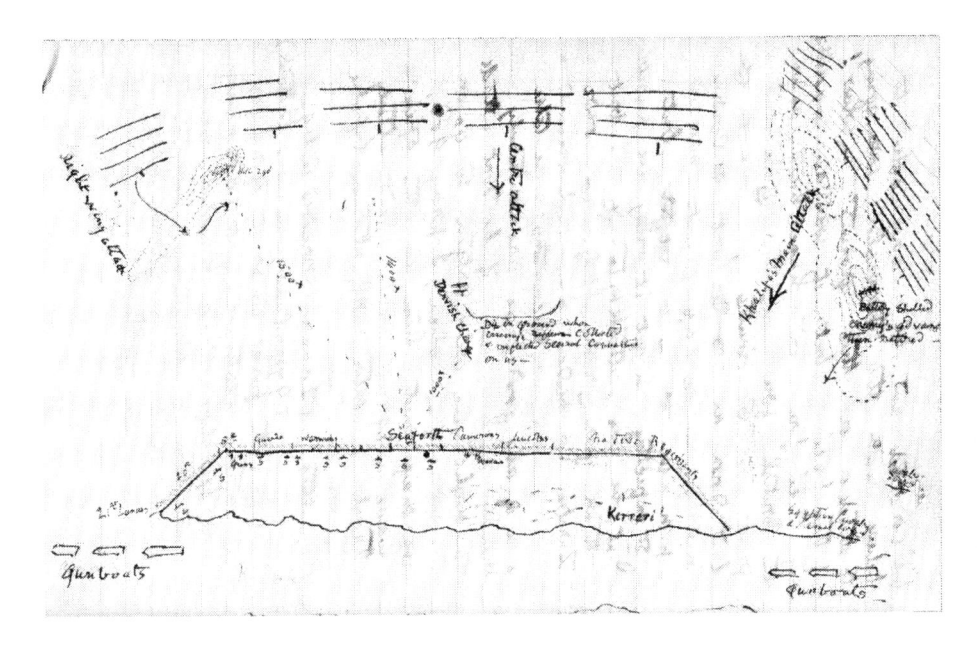

Teddy's map of the Battle of Omdurman

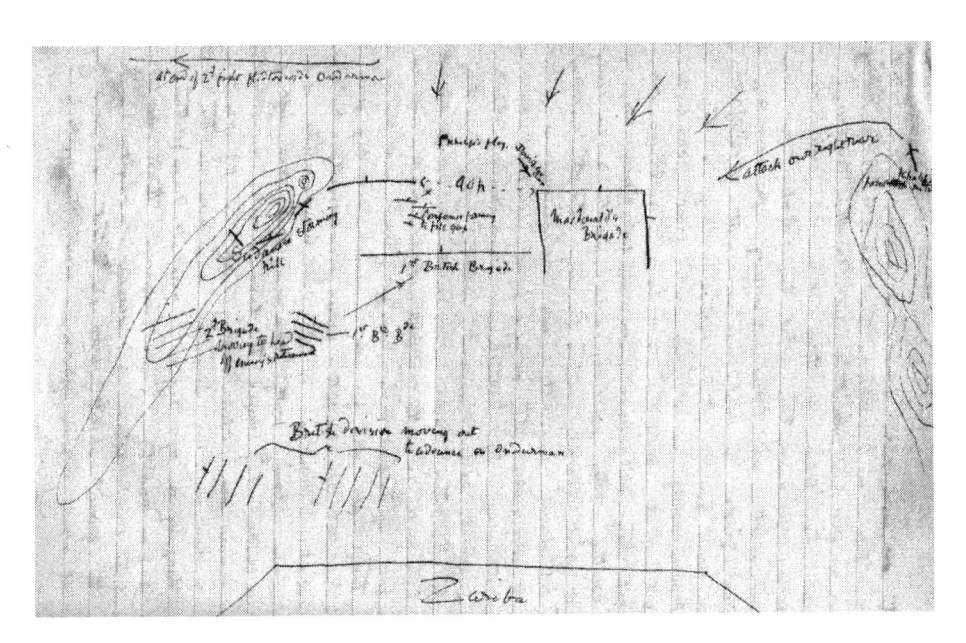

Teddy's map of the second action at Omdurman

From the Frontline of History

Chapter 6 The Legacy of the Sudan Campaign

It is interesting to note that there is no questioning or self-doubt expressed in the diary. He was young, certainly, and out to make a career, but it is striking that he never questions the necessity of the mission, despite this diary being intended very much for private use. Unlike the Crete diary which was kept by a group of officers, this diary was Teddy's alone, although he did allow Egerton to read it at a later date and write comments in the margin.

Today, it is easy to look back on the Sudan Campaign as an example of the arrogance of Empire, of Britain ruthlessly expanding its territory and using its technological and military advantage to crush its opponents. With the perspective of well over a century, we can perhaps see more clearly what was not evident to observers at the time. However, on reading the diary one is struck that triumphalist expansionism is never mentioned or even inferred. In fact, there is a sense of mission to 'free' Sudan from the oppressive rule of the Dervishes, who had seemingly devastated much of the countryside and abused her citizens. This may well have been informed by propaganda, but there are several interesting passages during the campaign where Teddy contemplates the land and conditions of the people, and evokes a sense of duty in their mission:

> *Both banks thick jungle and occasional villages which usually look in a rather dilapidated deserted state. Near each village – and in fact all along - can be seen old signs of cultivation. All the land must formerly have been richly cultivated until Mahdism and Dervish rule has frightened or killed everyone out of the country.*

And on his return to Cairo after the completion of his mission, he ruminates on the future for Sudan:

> *How long will it take the country to recover remains to be seen. It has been so terribly devastated & depopulated by this horrible Mahdist rule that I fear it may take some time before the country can be got into order.*

Teddy does make reference to *"wiping out"* the dishonour of the killing of General Gordon, and for the battle of Abu Klea which, together with the Abu Kru action two days later, had delayed the relief mission to Khartoum to rescue Gordon.

> *...well we have wiped all Abu Klea & Gabat, Tamai and El Tebs out and have wiped out Mahdiism, but it will take a long time for this country to recover, and in the meantime it will be a great expense.*

Interestingly, the facts of Abu Klea don't really seem to favour the Dervishes, with their casualties being over 1,100 dead, while British forces lost only 75; but it had entered popular consciousness as part of the failure of Gordon's mission which led to Mahdist rule dominating the Sudan for the next 15 years.

From the Frontline of History

Perhaps the death in the battle of Colonel Burnaby, who had achieved national fame with his exploits in Central Asia, and in particular his book A Ride to Khiva, had also shaken national confidence. In any case, the Battle of Abu Klea was immortalised in the famous imperial poem Vitai Lampada written by Sir Henry Newbolt in 1892:

> ...The sand of the desert is sodden red,
>
> Red with the wreck of a square that broke;
>
> The Gatling's jammed and the Colonel dead,
>
> And the regiment blind with dust and smoke.
>
> The river of death has brimmed his banks,
>
> And England's far, and Honour a name,
>
> But the voice of the schoolboy rallies the ranks,
>
> "Play up! play up! and play the game!"

Given that Teddy would have been an impressionable youth of 18 or 19 when Newbolt published the poem, it is interesting to speculate whether it had a particular resonance for him, given its allusions to cricket in the opening verse, and the famous exhortation to "play up! and play the game!".

From the Frontline of History

Teddy's views on the Campaign's leadership

What we do know is that some of the views he expresses about the leadership of the expedition are surprisingly negative, particularly when discussing the relentless picquet duty which he felt wore the men down unnecessarily. He had no time for Major General Gatacre, who is described in very unflattering terms, with Gatacre's approach to picquet duty coming in for particular criticism, especially when compared with the approach of the more experienced Egyptian Army:

> *And what does the Egyptian army, who have men experienced in Soudan warfare in authority, what do they do? Sleep comfortably – each battalion in line with only five men and a corporal as picquet behind the zariba. And we, with the same frontage, use 56 men up for 2 hours at a time against their five and do our men know all this? Of course they do and equally of course they must recognise the futility incompetency and infantile childishness of our tactics – Ours? No! General Gatacre's – to you Dear Diary I confide these things, because I may not speak them.*

Teddy's view was not unique, as Gatacre was known as 'Back-acher' in the army due to the punishing demands he made of his men. He may well have gone down in history as one of the prominent leaders of the campaign, but he was heartily disliked by those under his command:

> *Oh! Why! How! Is the British army burdened by incompetent asses like General Gatacre – Ach! Idiot.*

And:

> *Gatacre talked a lot of slush after the sermon this morning – he is mad.*

Teddy even muses on the prospect of Gatacre being captured and decapitated, such is his dislike of him:

> *....as we have some knowledge of our gallant General's lunatic tendencies. The report is that a party of dervishes are advancing down the river and are nearly certain to meet Backacher going up – The Bugler's face will look rather funny on a stick at Khartoum.*

Other members of the senior British leadership are also subject to wry comment – with Slatin Pasha[38] described somewhat sarcastically as *"Simply covered in medals"* even in the middle of the Sudan!

Teddy wasn't alone in his criticisms, with Egerton writing to his mother[39]:

> *General Gatacre who I look on as a mad fool....*

More positively, Teddy thought highly of General Wauchope, who would go on to be killed during the Boer War, while Kitchener, the leader of the expedition

---

[38] Otherwise known as Major-General Rudolf Anton Carl Freiherr von Slatin, Geheimrat, GCVO KCMG CB – an Anglo- Austrian soldier and administrator in the Sudan
[39] Egerton Archive - M.1994.112.84

under the grandiose title of Sirdar[40], was criticised for being over-confident at Omdurman. Teddy felt that the second attack of the Khalifa's forces, which placed the British troops under some pressure for a time, could have been avoided if Kitchener had been more circumspect. Teddy credits the Sudanese and Egyptian troops for standing firm; without their resolve, the British could have suffered much more significant losses.

When one thinks of any campaign like the Sudan Campaign, one tends to focus mainly on the key battles – undoubtedly moments of high drama and personal risk - the moments that could make a soldier's career or end his life. The excitement that Teddy feels when he hears in the Officer's Mess in Cairo that they are to mobilise and head upriver is palpable. War and conflict brought opportunity, as he later expresses in his Boer War diary, during the course of which he saw more limited action and certainly no set piece battles of the scale of Omdurman:

> ...dangers mean chances, and both mean advancement...

For career soldiers, these moments are undoubtedly the ones they look back on as pivotal events in their professional lives, and they obviously hold great interest for us. However, what strikes one about the Sudan Campaign is the sheer logistical effort that went into it. For Teddy to get from Cairo to the main camp at Darmali on the Nile, he had to travel nearly 1,500 miles by boat, train, camel and on foot. Simply to keep the British troops supplied was a huge

---

[40] Sirdar was the official title of the British Commander-in-Chief of the Anglo-Egyptian army and was also used by the Ottomans to refer to a Commander-in-Chief

undertaking. The Campaign included the building of a railway at lightning pace to carry troops and supplies deep into the heart of Sudan, and this showed the level of commitment and planning of the British: a commitment that in 1898, at the height of its Imperial power, meant that Britain could also brook no failure.

Of course, the battles were only a tiny part of the overarching campaign: the Battle of Atbara for example commenced at 06.20 a.m. and was all over by 08.30 a.m.; and yet Teddy was on campaign from 27 February until 17 September, for six and a half months of relentless heat and discomfort. Keeping the troops motivated in the face of boredom was a full-time job and his diary features Brigade marches and firing exercises, as well as more amusing interludes such as Gymkhanas and inter-regimental sports. These may sound to our ears to be no more than jolly japes in the desert, but they served the very real function of keeping soldiers motivated, fit and engaged, as well as promoting their Esprit de Corps. Nonetheless, there were also moments of intense frustration, when the Expeditionary forces wanted to have at the enemy just to get the job done.

It is amazing how quickly the troops, and in particular the Seaforths, were moved out of Sudan after the Battle of Omdurman. They had, of course, been on campaign for a long time, and were overdue some rest and relaxation. Even so, less than a week after the last shot was fired, they were on gyassas sailing down the Nile. The whole campaign had lasted six months, so its sudden ending must have felt strange, although Teddy was delighted by the availability of even the simplest food and drink as he made his way closer to Cairo. In the end, the contact with the enemy was short, sharp and decisive. There was plenty of danger and risk, and not just from a Dervish bullet or spear, but also from disease and the elements. During the First World War, Teddy's prolonged exposure to combat would be far more prolonged and while there was little in the way of decisive action, the constant pressure of ever-present danger was certainly very debilitating. However, that was still a long way into the future and much water was to pass under the bridge before then, not least the different but very real dangers of the second Boer War.

From the Frontline of History

Chapter 7 Teddy returns to active service in the second Boer War

Following the conclusion of the Sudan Campaign diary, we have no documentary evidence for what Teddy did over the next two years other than a brief recap that he gives at the beginning of the Boer War diary, with the following breakdown:

- Cairo '99
- Abyssinia, 1 Oct 99 / April 1900
- Cairo
- Hythe, August / September 1900
- ADC 2/B Aldershot, Oct 1900 – Nov 1901
- Sailed for South Africa, 7 Nov 1901
- Burghersdorp, Dec 1901, active service

Most intriguingly, perhaps, is the reference to Abyssinia as it seems likely this was part of an official mission – it lasted for seven months – but I can find no record of it to date. The British had been much involved with the Abyssinian Emperor Menelik, who had been fending off the European powers circling his Empire. He had defeated the Italians at the Battle of Adowa in 1896, but the French and the British were still a threat, and the Khalifa in Khartoum was hardly an ally – the Mahdists had killed the previous Emperor Yohannes IV at the Battle of Metemma in March 1889.

The French had sent a mission to Fashoda (modern day Kodok in South Sudan), where some of the Mahdist forces had fled after the Battle of Omdurman, and Kitchener moved there to pressure the French to leave after the battle in September 1898. After some polite posturing between Kitchener and the French Commander Captain Jean-Baptiste Marchand, the French withdrew through Abyssinia. Teddy briefly mentions Fashoda in his diary, stating that he was sorry not to have gone on there as part of the mission, writing on 8 September 1898:

> *I should very much have liked to have taken part in the expedition to Fashoda. Andrew Murray, three subalterns & 100 men of the Camerons are going.*

He also speculates over the prospect for big game hunting if he had gone.

Emperor Menelik was also obliged to contend with the Dervish influence in the Ogaden, in what is modern-day Somaliland. In particular, Menelik was concerned by the rise of Mohammed Abdullah Hassan, the so-called Mad Mullah. He had started to come to prominence in 1897, and since that date had been buying arms from the French and raiding tribes friendly to the British, as well as attacking Ethiopian forces. By April 1899 he had amassed 3,000 tribesmen, and soon thereafter declared Jihad[41] which attracted many more followers. It was clear that he was setting himself up in the image of the Khalifa and the Mahdi in order to promote war against the infidel and force them out of Somaliland.

The Mad Mullah's followers clashed with Abyssinian forces in March 1900 at Jijiga, and although they were repulsed, Menelik became very nervous at how the situation was developing. He approached Lieutenant Colonel Sir James Hayes Sadler K.C.M.G., C.B., F.R.G.S., the Consul-General of the British Protectorate on the Somali Coast, with a view to sending a joint military expedition in late 1900[42]. This request ultimately led to the 1901 mission by Lt-Col. Eric John Eagles Swayne who commanded a force of Somali soldiers which, in conjunction with an Ethiopian army, attacked the Dervish forces.

Given Teddy's experience fighting the Dervishes at Omdurman and Atbara is seems entirely possible that he was part of the initial mission. There were also discussions between Menelik and the British over the location of the western Abyssinian border with Sudan and it is equally possible that he was attached to a mission to discuss this, or that he joined one of the several geographical and nature expeditions that traversed Abyssinia in 1899/1900. We have no way of knowing, although he does describe the period as part of his military

---

[41] Mad Mullah of Northern Somaliland by Robert Hess, Journal of African history, V3 (1964) pp 415-433
[42] http://kaiserscross.com/188001/333222.html

career, rather than extended leave, but he also does not categorise it as active service.

One final possibility is reflected in an intriguing reference in the Aberdeen Press and Journal from September 1899[43] which states:

> A detachment of about 200 men of the 1st Battalion Seaforth Highlanders is expected to be sent to Khartoum in October, and will probably remain there until the spring of next year. The Sirdar considers a British garrison for Khartoum necessary, in view of the forthcoming expedition by the Egyptian and Soudanese troops into Kordofan in pursuit of the Khalifa and the remainder of his dervish army.

However, Kordofan is to the South West of Khartoum and it seem unlikely that Teddy would have described this as Abyssinia. He is also not listed as an officer in Egerton's account of his occupation of Khartoum, so he certainly didn't accompany Egerton in this instance.

Having returned from Abyssinia to Cairo, where the 1st Battalion were based, he spent the next few months there. The 1st Seaforths had fully expected to be sent out to South Africa to join the 2nd Battalion, who had been sent out at the start of the Boer War. However, with the situation in Egypt precarious, they

---

[43] Aberdeen Press and Journal - 20 September 1899

were considered indispensable and had to remain there given their knowledge and experience of the situation locally.

Teddy's record then states that he was posted as aide-de-camp to Colonel (temporary Major-General) R.H. Murray C.B., C.M.G, commanding the Second Infantry Brigade at Aldershot, where he spent a year between October 1900 and November 1901. Colonel Murray had commanded the 1st Battalion Seaforth Highlanders during the Sudan Campaign and must have thought highly of Teddy as a young, up-and-coming officer to take him with him to Aldershot[44]. It is possible that the posting was also due to his family connections with the Royal Sussex Regiment, which made up part of the Brigade.

At this time, Teddy transferred from the 1st Battalion to the 2nd Battalion Seaforth Highlanders. Why did he do this? Was he keen to fight in the Boer War following the murder of his brother Charlie after the Battle of Vlakfontein on 29 May 1901, and consequently requested this transfer? Although he never speaks of a desire for vengeance, this may have played some part in his decision, or perhaps he simply wanted to play his own part in the war. What is more likely is that active service was the way to promotion and opportunity, as he himself had said. While the role of A.D.C. at Aldershot was prestigious, Teddy wasn't by nature a pen-pusher. He very much craved active service as a

---

[44] Interestingly, Murray and Egerton did not get along at all well, as he relates to his mother in a letter from Sudan: *"Our Colonel continues to lead us a perfect dog's life, nag nag nag all day ....He never can let anyone do his job, he always thinks that he can do it a bit better."* Egerton Archive - M.1994.112.84

way of securing advancement. His promotion to the rank of Captain on 19 March 1901, was something that Teddy explicitly credits to 'Brother Boer':

> *A Captain in under six years' service is indeed luck and I have to thank Brother Boer for it.*

His promotion was, therefore, before the murder of his brother. Was it simply due to the losses that the 2nd Battalion Seaforth Highlanders had sustained at their earlier battles in the war? Very possibly, although those had occured several years previously. What seems more likely is that a new military innovation which came to prominence during the Boer War required fresh talent to build and lead it, namely – the Mounted Infantry.

The Mounted Infantry, or MI, were, as the name suggests, infantry who moved around on horseback. They were not a substitute for cavalry and would never fight from horseback but were trained in infantry tactics. The MI were a relatively new development for the British Army, and really came in to their own in South Africa, where the great distances made marching slow and impracticable. The speed and manoeuvrability of the Boer forces was one of their great strengths, and the traditional British Army units had struggled to keep up. As we have seen, the volunteer MI units of the Imperial Yeomanry – such as the Ceylon Mounted Infantry in which Teddy's brother Charlie had served – had been recognised by the British High Command for their usefulness from their first deployment in South Africa in early 1900, but they were very few in number and had taken many casualties.

From the Frontline of History

In January 1901, the War Office in Edinburgh had ordered the creation of a Scottish Mounted infantry Battalion[45]. These men were to be drawn from the Royal Scots Fusiliers, the Royal Highlanders (Black Watch), and the Seaforth Highlanders. From this order, it may be understood that the War Office intended to send a battalion of Scottish mounted infantry to South Africa, and Teddy clearly meant to be among them. According to Egerton, over the next two years, the majority of the drafts from the 1st Battalion Seaforths that were sent to South Africa would be to the Mounted Infantry.

With capable volunteer recruits becoming harder to find as the war went on, at the end of 1901 the regular Army trained a new force of 7,000 MI to go out to South Africa, led by professional officers. Indeed, while Teddy was serving at Aldershot, there was a significant body of nearly 700 MI drawn from the Grenadiers, Coldstreams, Scots and Irish Guards, King's Liverpool Regiment, Essex Regiment, 2nd Highland Light Infantry, 3rd Manchester Regiment and 4th Worcester Regiment being trained[46] and they were ordered to embark for South Africa just after Teddy's own departure to the war.

Teddy would therefore have been very familiar with the concept and methods of the MI and, given his horsemanship and battle experience from Sudan, would have been an obvious candidate to join this new venture. It seems to have also secured his promotion to Captain, a rank that he would hold for the next 13 years.

---

[45] Dundee Courier, 26 January 1901
[46] Worcestershire Chronicle, 09 November 1901

From the Frontline of History

The Origins of the Boer War

The Boer War came at the end of the so-called Scramble for Africa, in which rival European colonial powers vied with each other for control over Africa's resources. Although the British Cape Colony was established in 1795, and was confirmed after the Anglo-Dutch Treaty of 1814, it was built on a much older Dutch East India Company colony founded in 1652. The British had ceded self-government to the Colony in 1872. The real trouble had started after Cecil Rhodes became Prime Minister of the Cape Colony in 1890. With his ambition and hunger for resources, he made the Afrikaner (Boer) populations of the Orange Free State and the Transvaal nervous that he coveted their land. Sure enough, in 1895 the infamous Jameson Raid took place, in which 500 British adventurers tried to seize Johannesburg in the hope of triggering an uprising by the non-Boer 'uitlanders', who felt they had been denied their rights. This failed to happen, largely due to the poor execution of the raid, and the participants were soon rounded up by forces under Piet Cronje.

While the failure of the raid led to the removal of Rhodes as Prime Minister, the Boers were more wary than ever. The discovery of gold and diamonds only added fuel to the fire and although the Boer War did not actually break out until 11 October 1899, the Boer forces had spent the intervening years in preparation, not least in making an alliance between the Orange Free State and the Transvaal.

In the first phase of the war, the 2nd Battalion Seaforth Highlanders had been heavily engaged, fighting both at Magersfontein (1899), a terrible defeat for the British which saw the Highland Brigade take 747 casualties, including the death of their commander General Wauchope[47], and then at Paardeberg (1900), which was again a hugely costly battle for the British. By the time that Teddy arrived in December 1901, these set piece battles had given way to a campaign of guerrilla warfare and commando raids, and this had required a drastic change of tactics on the part of the British. This included the construction of some 8,000 blockhouses and 3,700 miles of wire fencing guarded by 50,000 troops[48]. These were combined with a scorched-earth policy, and were intended to break the ability of the highly mobile Boer Commando to roam freely and attack British forces.

Teddy's participation in the Boer War would be very different to his experience in the Sudan and Crete. No longer was he part of a large-scale army manoeuvring an enemy into a set piece battle as in the Sudan, or peacekeeping between two rival communities in Crete. In South Africa, the British were facing a highly organised and well-resourced enemy, which had the latest weapons and the training to use them. If Omdurman had been the last major set piece battle of the 19th century, the Boer War displayed many elements that would become features of 20th century wars – accurate, rapid-firing weapons including machine guns, high-explosive shells, highly mobile forces deploying hit-and-run tactics, and the first general use of concentration camps. While the British Army had been fine-tuned for the smaller colonial wars that

---

[47] General Wauchope was highly thought of by Teddy during the Sudan Campaign
[48] https://www.angloboerwar.com/boer-war

made up most of the 19th century conflicts after Waterloo, its shortcomings became rapidly obvious in its disastrous early defeats by the Boers.

Teddy's deployment to South Africa was late in the campaign, and the end of the war was already in sight. His posting at Aldershot had doubtless been prestigious, but it had also meant that he had missed the worst of the fighting. His time in South Africa is divided into two distinct phases. In the first, he was on blockhouse duty in the Eastern Transvaal, building and guarding the railway line that the British had used to successfully contain the Boers. It was largely dull work, enlivened only by the potential for polo and cricket. The second and more interesting part was his time spent in the Mounted Infantry.

Teddy was demonstrably a very fine horseman, and his diary in Sudan documents his horse-riding abilities and love of polo; the MI would have been a natural place for him. Interestingly, his brother Charlie had also shared those skills and put them to good use in some of the earliest MI units in the Boer War, serving in both the Ceylon Mounted Infantry and the Imperial Yeomanry. Teddy seems to have enjoyed his time in the MI and certainly doesn't complain about tactics and the army hierarchy as he did at other times. He was an active man, and seemingly enjoyed the great outdoors and big horizons of the veldt, in contrast to the duller blockhouse duty.

His diary is much less fulsome that either Sudan or Crete, and as an older and more experienced officer he is less light-hearted. When nothing is happening, he doesn't feel the need to fill the void. However, he does allow himself a more reflective introduction and conclusion and these offer us a rare insight into his thinking. The introduction in particular is very prescient and poignant:

Dear Diary

Oh chronicler of the great deeds of the only living E.C! What pride must be thine! Thou art cheap – too cheap – 3/ did I pay for thee and thou art like to be handed down to future generations, when the biography of the great E.C is written – then wilt thou be eagerly devoured. Yea - in future years, when the writer of these poor words is but dust and ashes and food for the worms! Then wilt thou be seized upon by the historian to record the deeds - thoughts and loves! of this great man that is to be, but is not as yet.

Vanity - vanity - conceit – conceit - more like art thou to be read through by some perchance sorrowing sister or wife or friend - who sorrows not so much for the man, but for a life ill spent, for chances neglected. A life that has been thrown away in the worldly amusement and which has never turned itself into seriousness but which has wandered through the world in idleness, taking life easily denying itself nothing. A man who can look back on many, many pleasant memories, who has done little or no good to anyone. A man with plenty of friends, but few real ones.

Ah, well my dear diary! It may be the former, but I fear it will be the latter type you will chronicle. A type easily popular, but one that does few good deeds. A type mourned when dead for a day, forgotten tomorrow!

Yet why, if your author find that there be danger of his life being of the latter type, does he not say with determination and vigour? "I will not. It is of the first type of man I will try to be." Ah! One makes many resolutions in this versatile life. So many, that perchance one fears making another yet another, that in the future may be broken.

Thus dear diary we will leave it to you, that by the written pages herein, may perhaps be found something of good - an undercurrent of a decent life.

Yet you are an open book - a book that all may read, who may find time that they feel they can waste it. Therefore but little of any depth of private ideas, of aspirations, of success, of fallen hopes, can appear in thy pages. So nought will be found, but a light record of doings and of people your author meets - which may be of interest to E.C., if he ever lives to be old enough to take pleasure in refreshing his memory by glancing through your pages, or, if before usual span of life, he goes elsewhere - to hunt in Mars - to kiss in Venus - to be thirsty in a hot place – or wherever he may go. Then perchance you, my dear diary may be of interest to the dear ones your author will leave in this world!

It is almost as if he knows that his diary will be subjected to the scrutiny of future generations. As it was, the diary was indeed kept by one of his sisters after his death and has passed down through the generations. Again, it is almost as if he suspects that fate and fears it, as he pulls back from full disclosure to state *"Yet you are an open book….so nought will be found but a light record of doings and people your author meets."* Indeed, nowhere does he record the *"loves"* that he alludes to, or anything of the more personal nature.

At this stage he was in his late 20s - twenty eight to be precise - and had quite recently been promoted to Captain, his second promotion in five years. However, he was not to rise above this rank for the next 13 years, reflecting the limited potential for career progression in peacetime. In the Crete diary, we read of Teddy's 'cheek' that made him fun to be around and was indulged by his senior officers. However, we also now can read Teddy reflecting on:

> *A life that has been thrown away in the worldly amusement and which has never turned itself into seriousness but which has wandered through the world in idleness, taking life easily denying itself nothing.*

For a twenty-eight-year-old who has already been on two tours of active duty, and about to start a third, and who has been promoted twice, this would seem unduly harsh. But it reflects an underlying vulnerability that surfaces on several occasions: that his humour and light-heartedness has stood in the way of his career progression, that he hasn't been taken seriously. As a younger son he had very little money and is always complaining about running short: he needed a successful career to set himself up in life. He also had the example of the successful ancestors that would have surrounded him in the many pictures that lined the walls of Danny, his childhood home; and that is not even to mention his mother and her many good works – maybe he felt inadequate by comparison.

When Teddy arrived in South Africa, he was almost immediately posted to blockhouse duty in the Burghersdorp district of the Eastern Transvaal. He seems to have divided his time between the Burghersdorp region and the area around modern-day Pretoria, including Wonderboom Bridge and Stromberg, and the Lydenburg district, including Badfontein and Witkliff to the East of Pretoria. What is surprising is that these are all quite a distance from each other, with Burghersdorp being 450 miles from Pretoria. However, thanks to a well-established railway service, he seems to have been able to cover the distance rapidly and is frequently shuttling between the two areas.

On one of these journeys on the 14 December 1901, he recounts an amusing anecdote which must have befallen every kilted solider at some point[49]:

> *Came back on the mail train and jumped out at Wonderboom, where I was ass enough to alight on my head, my kilt over my back and altogether made a real fool of myself. However, this is not the first time. I fancy a few of the passengers had a very good view of a certain part of EC's beautiful person.*

The blockhouses were principally built to protect the railway network from the hit and run tactics of the Boers. Initially the blockhouses were very substantial

---

[49] As is traditional, kilted regiments wore no underwear

constructions, more like miniature castles. But these were time consuming and expensive to build and given the vast open spaces of South Africa, it was not practical to rely on this approach. Instead, Major Spring Rice of the Royal Engineers[50] had devised a new system where the walls were made using two layers of corrugated iron sheets infilled with shingle. These cost a fraction of the price of the more substantial blockhouses, and yet were still effective against rifle fire. Consequently, the blockhouse building programme mushroomed and with barbed wire strung between the outposts, the ability for the Boer Commando to move was increasingly curtailed.

Much of the blockhouse duty was dull, largely consisting of overseeing their construction and complaining about the lack of materials. Very little of any interest happens in December 1901 and January and February 1902: for the most part, Teddy builds blockhouses and plays polo and cricket.

On 8th of January there is some excitement as there was news of Boers:

> *My native scout reported to me in the afternoon that there were four Boers on Prulofsi's farm – took out eight men, Macan and two natives. Great tactics displayed and house successfully surrounded without loss of a single man. Great bravery displayed by all – a dashing charge on the house, fixed bayonets – beautiful.*

---

[50] http://samilitaryhistory.org/vol136rs.html

From the Frontline of History

> *No Boers - one woman and child, one native woman and child. Searched house, in oven – no one – return crestfallen, hot and angry.*

The Boers were proving elusive, but the British blockhouse strategy was beginning to hem them in and make their free movement much more difficult. While Teddy may have found that frustrating, it was evidence that the strategy was working. As Teddy relates in his diary:

> *There is nothing of interest dear diary to record in you from the above date until the great E.C. got orders to leave Burghersdorp. A certain amount of polo, which I enjoyed madly, though bar the first time played poorly.*

On 18 January he heard there was some chance of his relocating, and on Monday 20th January he learned that his men were to be relieved by 6/ Worcesters. He remarks on their youth and inexperience which brought its own risks in the tense standoff now occurring:

> *….relieved by the 6/ Worcesters, who look terribly young and inexperienced, mere children in fact, with the result that they are very jumpy and I have heard that in the first 10 days through carelessness and jumpiness they have manged to kill two and wound eight of their own men.*

On Friday 24 January they moved from Burghersdorp to Bloemfontein and then onto Kroonstad where they detrained late on Sunday evening. Here the Seaforths continued to build blockhouses ahead of a planned 'drive', in which the British were trying to ensnare the highly effective forces of Christiaan de Wet, the Boer General, against the blockhouse line. The 'drive' itself was a complex and challenging operation, involving a 60-mile line of British mounted troops pushing forward at a rate of over ten miles a day, often for a week at a time. At night, strong picquets would be placed to ensure no Boers could slip through the net. The first drive lasted between the 5-8 February and Teddy was in position to play his part:

> *The drive began today, several columns are to attempt to drive the Boers into the triangle of Kroonstad – Pretoria line and Hilbrau / Wolvehoek, they all started off this morning, early, but seemed to be going very slowly as by 1 p.m. they were still in sight. They believe they have De Wet and 2,000 Boers in the cordon.*

While Teddy does not see any action during this drive, there is no doubt that this new strategy played an important role in forcing the Boers to the negotiating table. By restricting their freedom of movement, even over the huge open spaces of South Africa, the effectiveness of the Boer units was significantly reduced. Over the rest of February and early March, a series of drives broke up De Wet's force.

For Teddy though, his war was about to change and, on 20 February, he received a wire telling him to report to Pretoria for Mounted Infantry duty, upon which he formally joined the 2 Coy 18th Mounted Infantry on the 29 February.

For the next few months, he helped guard the convoys into Lydenberg but there seems to have been very little to do, the war was almost over. On the 3rd of May he writes:

> *There has been nothing of much interest my dear diary to write in you during the last month. The Boogers steadily refuse to attack the Lydenberg convoy, a good deal no doubt due to the excellent dispositions made by the great E.C. Especially on one occasion, when there was no doubt they meant to attack only E.C was in command of a '[***] Force' and so splendid were the tactics displayed that the enemy thought discretion the better part of valour.*
>
> *The column has been at Shoeman's Kloof for the last month and has only a few days ago moved to Helvetia. The great event has been the pleasant prospect of peace being at last a solid fact. We all hope and long for it. Well another 12 days should settle it one way or the other.*

But the war was not altogether over for Teddy and in fact one of his more demanding treks started on the 8 May when he trekked 26 miles to Paardeplaats. He saw a few Boers on what appeared to be an immensely strong position, but they withdrew in the face of the British force threatening to encircle them.

The next day was to bring more contact with Boer forces, and we can read his first in depth description of an action against this mercurial foe:

On rear guard to column with 35 Coys & men. All the other mounted troops, except 25 men on each flank, moved off early at 5 a.m. for a combined movement. Gough from Lydenburg with national scouts cooperating.

At 5.30 a.m. I took up a position in rear of convoy and waited until it moved off – the last waggon did not get off until about 7.30 a.m. A few Boers rode across our front moving north. We then moved back to ridge over drift after the last waggon had crossed.

Sent a message to Sergeant MacKenzie to keep eight scouts in rear extending about ½ mile south of road and to send another four scouts to my right. Sent orders to keep supports handy and not to allow scouts to be too widely extended owing to the particularly difficult country we had to traverse.

Continued to move back slowly after the infantry rear guard.

Saw two farms on my left – one I thought occupied by about eight Boers. Left two subsections to cover retreat and visited first farm containing women who stated the further farm to be occupied only by kaffirs & also said there were plenty of chickens in it.

Decided not to raid 2nd farm and retired onto a hill. The only position as far as I could see that if we were attacked would allow the comfortable passage of draft by convoy and easy retirement of guns and infantry. Had hardly arrived before Boers, about 30 of them, rode down on ridge directly overlooking the 2nd farm. Lucky for me, Clarke, and the eight men I had taken with me, that we were not led into the trap evidently prepared.

Boers opened fire as soon as they could – not very heavy, but their shooting very good only a little high. We returned fire, which stopped them a bit.

It took about ¾ of an hour for last waggon to clear the drift. Then 15 minutes for guns, then ½ hour for infantry and then we left by degrees and galloped very fast along the road heading to drifts and occupied right and left of road the further side

The Boers followed onto our old position before we won over the drift. They seemed to be trying my left a good deal – so I soon retired again. They now appeared in some force on my right rear and got busy with Sergeant Mackenzie and Sergeant Clarke. Gave me a rather hot time from a farm. ¼ of an hour and returned again. My left seemed more secure but did not like the look of things on my right. Sergeant Mackenzie seemed however to be holding his own well, so kept my distribution of about 16 men in either side. It was just at this retirement that Private Groves was shot while holding Private Menzies and Shaw's horses. They had all in some way got separated from me. They were all captured. Groves badly hit through the left lung could not get away. We had retired very rapidly and neither of the men by any possibility could have gone in support as we had no sooner left our position than the Boers were on the next.

We next retired on to two hills forming a neck on each side of the road. My force on the left was fully exposed to Boer fire during this retirement, as I had to get round boggy ground. The fire was heavy but no casualties. So shooting must have been bad, due I believe to being well covered by fire from my force on right of road, who effected their retirement directly I was across the open zone of ground.

Took up a strong position (5th position) on each side of the road, saw convoy well on now. At about 12 noon made my last retirement into comparative security on ground commanding last drift and about one mile from camp. Sent back ambulance and got in Groves and the two captured men who looked supremely ridiculous in Boer clothes. Private Menzies looked fairly happy, at which I am not surprised when it afterwards transpired that he had concealed £150 about his person while taking off his clothes and putting on those of the Bougers and had also successfully hidden his rifle under a rock.

Am glad to say (rather to my surprise) that Col Curran commanding the Manchesters was good enough to compliment and thank me. The Manchester Infantry by their method of moving retarded me somewhat, but the men moved quickly and were in every way excellent.

From the Frontline of History

My own men were very steady and self-reliant. Clarke apparently thought the whole thing a funny joke. We did all retirements full gallop in a stream, men leaving positions by subsection. I found it necessary to be first away to lead the retirement, to select the next position and to prevent the danger of men galloping fast away from fire, the convoy getting out of hand and going too far, thereby pressuring the infantry and guns. A danger which is I am certain ever present even with the best MI in the world.

The Private Menzies that was taken prisoner says he saw a Boer knocked over and that the Boers on that flank numbered about 40, as there were some more in the rear and also further back towards the convoy there were a few snipers on the right. As I had personally seen about 30 riders down on my left at the commencement of the action, I think that the enemy must have numbered nearly 100.

The next two days were to see the last real action of Teddy's Boer War, with him raiding several farms, capturing a number of sheep and destroying large quantities of corn – Britain's scorched earth policy in action. On 10 May, the convoy he was guarding was severely attacked all day on the way to Dullstroom but seemingly without casualties and he covered about 40 miles over very hilly country.

The following day he returned to the Badfontein valley with the national scouts and raided a few farms, including one where he:

> *Saw a <u>lovely</u> girl at one and longed for the days of the saddle bow, only we should first of all have been digging holes in one another with rapiers to decide which would be the lucky man to carry off the lovely wench to camp.*

Over the next two weeks there would be further duty but no fighting and on the 1 June at 09.30 he heard the words that every soldier longs to hear: peace was declared. The war was over.

Teddy and the 18th Battalion Mounted Infantry moved into camp at Lydenburg where they waited for their orders to return home. Here he seems to have had a very enjoyable time with much sport, especially polo, a game that he would continue to play for the regiment to a very high standard in the next phase of his career:

> *Polo three times a week and nearly always good galloping games. The M.I are a right good sporting lot and ride hard. After we had been there a week there was a capital performance of the Belle of New York - considering the material really wonderfully good. We played cricket every Saturday, but we were a bad side and never by any sort of chance held a catch – made a few runs 13. 25. 40. 0.*

> *Played two football matches; 1st against the Sergeants, who turned up very confident - result 2 goals all. We ought to have won but got beat to the world. I personally never felt so ill in my life.*

From the Frontline of History

A very good boxing tournament at the end of June – took £50 at the door. Matthews was referee, self and Scott judges.

Teddy finally got his orders to leave on the 13th August and rode his trusty horse, the 'Rat', into Machadodorp, before heading on to Pretoria and Cape Town, where he stayed at the Mount Nelson Hotel. He complains about the expense all the way but seems to have had an enjoyable time. Nonetheless, it was with a sense of relief that he boarded the *Assaye* and set sail for home at 11 am Sunday morning, 31st August.

Teddy's reflections on the Boer War

At the end of the diary, Teddy records some reflections on the war and its organisation, and offers some poignant comments on the soldier's life and the value of home:

> *Well done diary, the short time is over, the game played and your author now counting the days, nay the very hours, that bring him nearer the old home. The home of his ancestors, the home where he was born, the home he loves.*

> *Perchance you may think it foolish of a soldier to hanker after home and all that it holds dear. Yet foolish or not the fact remains it is so; as we slowly grow to years of [some] discretion, be the amount small or great, the more when one leaves home to embark on some enterprise*

where danger lies does more one count up the chances for or against the likelihood of returning.

Thus when all danger is over and past, one returns again with a greater sense of thankfulness than when in years gone by one first set out with joy in one's breast to foreign climes and active service and never a thought of weighing the odds one way or the other: not dear diary that there has been any danger in this brief sojourn of ours, but there might have been.

Yet there must be feelings of regret that no more danger has been present, no chances forthcoming - dangers mean chances, and both mean advancement - so you dear diary will go on the shelf not much valued as no chances have been forthcoming and no advancement gained.

There are yet a few words to be added to your somewhat worthless pages and those are a few memories of the last months of the campaign that your author wishes to commit to memory and a few remarks on these last six months that will probably be read by him in future years and condemned as foolish.

Aside from complaining about the embarkation arrangements and the responsibilities placed on officers for the pay of their men, which he resented, he also alludes to the outrageous prices charged in the ship's canteen as well as the entraining arrangements. However, more interestingly, he comments on the British blockhouse strategy and on the Mounted Infantry itself:

Blockhousing

> The blockhousing system in Cape Colony appeared to me to be better than in any other part of the country. Better wired and more systematic, due no doubt to General French having got hold of all the wire that he required as it was landed at Cape Town. The system of fencing that prevailed in Cape Colony was to my mind very good and was copied in other parts of the country.
>
> The line between Kroonstadt and Lindley was badly wired. It was impossible to get enough wire. The blockhouses were excellently placed and there were enough of them. Had this line been anywhere near as strong as those in Cape Colony it would have taken all De Wet's cleverness to have got through. In fact, with good men in the blockhouses I doubt if he would have succeeded without suffering very heavy loss.

MI (Mounted Infantry)

> If there is one arm in this war that has covered itself with distinction I think everyone will admit that it is the MI, if they can be called an 'arm' in the service. Many were the men who predicted failure for infantry mounted on horses, saying they would forever be bad cavalry etc. Yet

what has been the result? The MI have never degenerated into bad cavalry and as long as they have no weapon for 'shock tactics' it is difficult to conceive why they should, so long as they do not emulate the bad example of many cavalry regiments.

The MI have had a lot to contend with: the worst horses, cavalry always having the pick; bad staff or rather untrained staff; C.Os who before had never in many cases commanded anything more than a company of infantry; officers many of whom know nothing about horses and in many cases totally untrained; a curious, and one might say a dangerous, class of fighting weapon to start in and throw into the field against the finest mounted infantry in the world.

Officers were appointed to the MI even though untrained, vied with one another in hard work and quickly adapted themselves to the extenuated circumstances.

Of course, in every regiment there were officers, who even if they did not know mounted infantry drill etc had been horse masters themselves and consequently soon taught the inexperienced ones horse management etc. So too with the men - force of circumstances soon welded the raw but splendid material & the whole result was, when peace was declared, a body of mounted rifles experienced in all their duties in the field, hard as nails, fit to go anywhere and 2nd to none. Not only that but far better than any other body of mounted rifles ever yet seen and one may safely assert ever will be seen again.

The MI have never been advertised nor have they ever advertised themselves. Their work has been quietly and well done and I do not think the MI were responsible for, or present at, many if any of the 'regrettable' 'incidents'; yet now the honour list is out, what have these hard worked officers – the COs of men who have made this glorious fighting weapon that surely finished the war? No one can say much – out of some 30 COs only five have been mentioned. It's the way of the world, but it is rather an unkind insult to the officers who welded and made this raw material into what it was at the close of hostilities…..

Finally, Teddy saves a few choice words for the apologists and supporters of the Boers in Britain:

Well dear Diary a few more 'grouses' and I will have finished. And there is a grouse that I cannot absent from your pages and that is the slack apathetic demeanour of the British public during the disgraceful speech meetings of the Pro-Boer traitors. The blackguardly traitors were allowed unmolested to make the most atrocious speeches and hold these disgraceful meetings to the detriment of the country as has now been proved to the continuance of the war. They have the blood of many brave officers and men, not at their doorstep but on their hands, and I trust that on the day of judgement they may be called to account. For they have as surely murdered as those who are tried for murder. Worse for they are both murderous and traitors and doubly base than the poor wretch who sticks a knife into his wife in a fit of temper or drunkenness.

Strong words indeed.

Teddy returned to Britain on the *Assaye*, presumably taking some well-earned leave. We next find him stationed back with the 1st Battalion Seaforth Highlanders in Cairo in 1902 in a photograph taken at the Kasr El-Nil barracks where the 1st Battalion were stationed, the 3rd Battalion being based at the Citadel. We have no material concerning his time in Cairo in 1902 – 1903, except for this photograph.

In October 1902, orders came through that the Seaforths were to be posted to India and in mid-February 1903 they arrived at Nasirabad where the next stage of Teddy's career would begin: one that was full of glittering achievement albeit sporting rather than military.

From the Frontline of History

Blockhouses and gardens at Wonderboom Bridge

Teddy in his blockhouse Christmas 1901

From the Frontline of History

Teddy on the veldt

Teddy at Wonderboom Bridge

Mounted infantry on the move

From the Frontline of History

Teddy, possibly on board The Rat

Teddy off duty

Chapter 8 Between wars: Teddy in India and Scotland

In 1903, the Seaforths were sent from their barracks at Kasr el-Nil to India, first to Nasirabad in Rajasthan and then in June 1905 to Nowshera in the north west of the Raj, near Peshawar in modern Pakistan. We have no diaries for this period and instead must follow Teddy's progress through reports of the polo or cricket matches in which he played. He seems to have embraced the lifestyle fully, buying and selling a string of polo ponies and even playing his only first-class cricket match in the prestigious Bombay Presidency game against the Parsees.

Teddy Campion was unquestionably a talented sportsman. All through his career, from his earliest days as a callow 2nd Lieutenant, to the very eve of the outbreak of the Great War, he played whatever sport was at hand - including bicycling, in which in August 1896 he came third in the Army Athletic Meeting's One Mile Bicycle Handicap.

First and foremost, Teddy was a prodigious cricketer, and cricket had a long heritage at Danny, Teddy's childhood home. Sand Field on the estate is the earliest identifiable cricket ground in the world, with the first recorded match being played in 1717. On receiving his commission in the Seaforths, Teddy almost immediately appears in the Regiment's cricket team and in July 1896 he was in the side that played Army College Heath End. This proved an inauspicious debut as, although he opened the batting, reflecting great confidence in his ability, he was out for a duck. A caricature exists of him at this time, dressed as a baby approaching the crease, bat and milk bottle in hand – the 'babe of the regiment'.

While he frequently played cricket during his Sudan and South African campaigns, the highlight of his cricketing career was certainly his only First Class Cricket appearance while he was serving with the Seaforth Highlanders in India. On 21 – 23 September 1903 he appeared for the Europeans against the Parsees in a Bombay Presidency match at the Deccan Gymkhana Ground at Poona (modern day Pune) – the most prestigious tournament of the Raj.

The Europeans won the toss and elected to bat. Despite the efforts of Cheetham, their opener, who made 30 runs, the wickets were falling rapidly before Teddy stepped up to the crease, batting at Six. He made a respectable 29 runs, the second highest score of the Europeans' first innings, before being bowled by K.S. Kapadia, who took six wickets for 27 runs that day. Teddy bowled three overs, including one maiden, for ten runs, but no wickets[51].

The correspondent of the Civil and Military Gazette[52] describes it thus:

---

[51] All cricket score information from www.cricinfo.com
[52] 30 September 1903

From the Frontline of History

Captain E. Campion of the Seaforth Highlanders (A batsman of the dashing order who had been scoring heavily in matches at Nasirabad, Indore and Mhow)....besides Cheetham, Campion was the only other man on the side who could do anything material in the way of increasing the score. This pair between them made 59 out of the total of 97. What the Presidency would have done without them it is difficult to say, but one thing is certain the innings would have been a fiasco.

In the second innings, he was bumped up the batting order to Four and made fourteen runs, the third highest of the Europeans, before being caught and bowled by Kekashru Mistry, who took four wickets that innings. The Parsees won by a crushing innings and six runs. Such was the only First Class Cricket match played by Teddy Campion – a very respectable effort.

Teddy's polo career

Having been brought up in a hard-riding household like Danny, Teddy was a considerable horseman. All through the Sudan Campaign and the Boer was he was always up for a horse race or a chukka of polo. By the time he arrived in India, he was a stalwart of the 1st Battalion's polo team and had contributed to its considerable success for many years.

Polo in India was a keenly contested inter-regimental sport, helped by the fact that even relatively impecunious officers like Teddy could keep the string of ponies that were needed to compete – something that would have been impossible in Britain. As one might expect, the Cavalry regiments had a natural advantage when it came to polo, but the Seaforths reputation preceded them to India from Cairo, where they had already been making waves.

It seems to be the general opinion among polo players that there has been no really first-rate British team in India of late such as would have had chance for the Inter-Regimental Tournament in a hot year, as, for instance, when the Durham Light Inf. or the 7th Hussars were at their best, A new light, however, has appeared on the horizon, which promises to grow very bright. The Seaforth Highlanders, stationed at Nusseerabad, arrived in India last February with a reputation made in Egypt, where they had won the Cairo Tournament having to meet the 11th Hussars in the finals; and they have just had chance of showing that, in spite of their comparatively short time in the country, they are formidable in any company. During the recent Mhow Week a couple of matches were arranged between them and the 10th Hussars, a team which gave a good account of themselves at the last Inter-Regimental Tournament. The result seems to have been a revelation to the spectators, for the Hussars were outplayed at all points of the game and beaten in the first match by eight goals to one, and in the second by four goals and four subsidiaries to two goals and one subsidiary. The appearance of a new team, and an infantry one at that, of such high promise, will give a great interest to the Regimental Championship at Meerut next spring. The team that played so strongly at Mhow consists of Capt. Campion (1), Mr. Buchanan (2), Mr. Maclachlan (3), and Capt. Carden (back).[53]

There were a series of major army polo competitions in India between February and March, with the Infantry Polo Cup followed a week later by the Inter-Regimental Cup. These were both held in Meerut, just outside Delhi, where the British Indian Army had one of its largest cantonments. The Seaforths were the new team in town, and everyone was keen to see how they were going to compete.

On the 26 February 1904, Teddy took to the field in the Infantry Polo Tournament with the Seaforths, playing in his favoured attacking position of 1. It was described thus by the Indian Daily News[54]:

> A very large gathering of spectators turned out to witness the concluding game in the above tournament, and they were fully rewarded by witnessing a fast galloping one, and though the Queens made a stout resistance, yet the strong combination of the Highlanders told on them from the very first commencement of the game....

And in the Army and Navy Gazette[55]:

> At Meerut, on the 26th February, the regimental team [Seaforths] won the Indian Infantry Polo Tournament. They met in the final contest the

---

[53] Homeward Mail from India, China and the East, 21 December 1903
[54] Indian Daily News - Thursday 03 March 1904
[55] Army and Navy Gazette - Saturday 19 March 1904

excellent team of the 1st Battalion Queen's Royal West Surrey Regiment. The Queen's made stout resistance, but it was plain from the outset that, good as their play was, they were quite outmatched. In the end, the Highlanders won the cup by four goals and one subsidiary to one goal and two subsidiaries. The teams were Queen's — Lieut. Alleyne (1), Lieut. Creek (2), Major Glasgow (3), and Capt. and Adjt. Mathew-Lannowe (back). Highlanders—Capt. Campion (1), 2nd Lieut. Maclachlan (2), Lieut. Buchanan (3), and Capt. Cardew (back). The ground was in perfect order, and the arrangements good as good could be. At the close of the play, Mrs. Henry, wife of Major-Gen. Henry, C.B., commanding the district, presented the cup, the winning team being much applauded, as it deserved to be.

A well-deserved victory then in his first major Indian polo tournament. However, following hard on its heels in April 1904 came the Inter-Regimental Competition, where the infantry had to play against cavalry regiments who had a natural advantage. A vivid account of the final is given in The Field[56]:

POLO. THE INTER-REGIMENTAL POLO WEEK AT MEERUT. THE BELL-RINGING for the teams of the Queen's and the Rifle Brigade to face each other signalled the opening of one of the largest and most interesting polo meetings held for many years past. For some years now polo in India has been at a low ebb, owing, of course, to the war and its consequences, and it was not till last year that a revival set in

---

[56] The Field, 9 April 1904

with the advent of the cavalry regiments from South Africa. In 1903 the 15th Hussars, with all the advantages of being quartered at Meerut, carried all before them, though narrowly escaping defeat from the 10th Hussars, who in sporting fashion came up to try, in spite of their having been a few months only in the country. Since that time ponies have been bought and trained in every part of India, and it was no surprise to find seven teams entered for the infantry tournament and nine for the inter-regimental the following week. It is not often that polo players have such a treat as to find fifteen regimental teams at the same station. The championship tournament, open to the world, is always put down to be played during the week after the regimental meeting........

……The 15th Hussars then faced the Seaforths. The latter had never had an opportunity of playing a really first-class team, and great interest was evinced to see how they would fare. They played a good, combined game, and in their No. 2, Mr Maclachlan, possess a player who can hit with deadly and almost invariable accuracy. The game had not been in progress many minutes before a terrific storm broke, and all further play was out of the question. It wasn't for three days that the elements allowed play to be resumed. Many of the soldiers had had to return to their stations, and the crowd of spectators was noticeably smaller, but keen interest was shown when the match between the 15th Hussars and the Seaforths was begun afresh on Tuesday, March 8. For the first five minutes the hopes of the Scotsmen ran high, as, playing well

From the Frontline of History

together, they ran up two goals and a subsidiary to one goal scored by their opponents. After that, however, the Hussars drew away, and never again being really pressed, they won a good fast game by seven goals to two.

Spurred on by this success, Teddy took it upon himself to try and revive the Rajputana and Central India Polo tournament, which had been in abeyance for several years. He became the Honorary Secretary and solicited teams to come and play. The tournament was to be played at Nasirabad in late October 1904 and was open to Rajastana, Central India, Deccan and Ahmedabad teams. The competitions were described in The Field[57]:

The Mhow Tournament had to be abandoned owing to plague, and the last tournament, commenced during the last week in October, was the Rajputana and Central reunion. That keen polo regiment the Seaforth Highlanders have revived the interest in this event, and it was hoped that six teams would come to the post, but unfortunately the Central India Horse, the 31st Lancers, and the 10th Hussars had to scratch, leaving the Poona Horse and Abu Gymkhana to dispute the ultimate result. The Poona Horse first met the 1st Seaforths, but the former did not place their strongest team in the field, while the Seaforths utilised the services of three officers who had shown sterling merit in previous competitions. The Poona horse were composed of Mr Grimshaw, Mr Black, Mr Norbery, and Capt. Newnham (back); the 1st Seaforths being

---

[57] The Field - 03 December 1904

represented by Mr Laverton, Capts. MacLachlan, Campion, and Carden (back). The Poona Horse led off with two goals, the Highlanders, however, pulling themselves together in the penultimate period, when they equalised. Mr MacLachlan was able to hit through for the Highlanders a few minutes before the final bell sounded, the team therefore winning a well-played contest by three goals to two.

The Abu Gymkhana then met the Seaforths in the final tie on Oct. 28, and no one could have desired a more exciting or keenly contested game. The Highlanders led for three periods by four goals to two, but their opponents in the next chukker strengthened their attacks, and made a tie of the contest at five goals all. For the last chukker only four minutes remained, and the Highlanders added two subsidiaries to their opponents' one, so they secured the cup of the Rajputana tournament by one subsidiary.

In June 1905, having once again reached the final of the Infantry Polo Cup, but on this occasion losing to the 2nd Battalion King's Royal Rifles, the Seaforths were obliged to transfer to Nowshera in the north west of the Raj, near modern day Peshawar[58]. Needless to say, that did not stop the polo, and several matches were reported in the newspapers over the next few years.

In January 1906, after six months at Nowshera, Teddy was seconded from the Seaforths to the Supply and Transport Corps, (Rawalpindi Division), and in early

---

[58] Civil & Military Gazette (Lahore) - 21 June 1905

From the Frontline of History

1907, perhaps in recognition of his eye for horse flesh, he was appointed to the officiating command of the 18th Mule Cadre. Teddy seems to have stopped playing for the main Seaforth polo team at this time, probably as he was now away from the regiment's base near Peshawar. He was recorded as playing only once for the regiment in 1906, against Rawalpindi Gymkhana, although he did play for the Hammerkop team against the 10th Hussars at the end of the year.

During 1906, Teddy also advertised a number of horses for sale in the local press. Whether he was horse trading to earn a little more money or selling down his ponies after having to leave the team is unknown.

His final moment of glory playing for the Seaforth polo team came in August 1907, when the Seaforths crushed the Native Cavalry during the Gulmarg Tournament by 11 goals to nil, before losing to the Guides in the final by one goal:

> *A large and enthusiastic crowd assembled to see the finals in anticipations of a close and well contested game were fully realised. The ground, though still heavy, was not so slippery as on the first day, and the play was excellent all through. Chukker.—From the throw in the Seaforths got quickly on and ran the ball down to the Guides' end and hit over the line. Campion met a weak throw in and scored first blood for the Seaforths...... The game was hotly contested all through these periods, the Seaforths hitting being especially clean and effective, but the defence on both sides was beyond reproach.... a further period*

> had to be played with widened goals. Some fast and furious play followed, but the Guides gradually forced the Seaforths back, and from a hot scrimmage in front of goal Davies got the ball through and won one of the finest games we have seen in any Gulmarg by the narrow margin of one goal.[59]

This seems to have been a fitting end to his competitive polo career and he is not recorded as having played in any further competitive matches for the Regiment. In March 1908, after just over a year with the 18th Mule Cadre, he sold off the last of his polo ponies and returned to the UK[60]. Initially, this was for six months on a medical certificate, but ultimately, he never went back to India. We do not know what the medical reason was, although in 1915, after he was gassed at Ypres, his sister Mary wrote stating her concerns for him:

> ....but one always feel that anything likely to affect his lungs is rather serious, on account of the attack of [Pneumonia? /illegible] which he had in India.

Unfortunately, it has not been possible to decipher her handwriting, but it is clear that he was sufficiently ill to be sent home and for a new post to be found for him in the healthier climes of the UK. It may also explain why the effects of gas in the Great War had such a long-lasting and ultimately fatal impact on him.

---

[59] Civil & Military Gazette (Lahore) - 31 August 1907
[60] In March 1908, the Civil and Military Gazette (Lahore) carried an advert for three polo ponies, Sweet Lady, Saunterer and a Bay Gelding, all of which were available at reduced prices as they were the property of Captain Campion who had gone home.

After his return to Britain there is no further mention of him playing polo. This is most likely due to the cost; keeping a string of ponies was affordable in India on a Captain's salary but would have been impossible in Britain[61]. However, there is no doubt that the highpoint of his sporting life came while he was serving in India, where there was seemingly plenty of spare time for polo and cricket.

Teddy comes to Scotland

While based in Edinburgh on his return to Britain (the first time he had actually been based in Scotland) in November 1908 he arranged an exchange with Captain C. Macfie, of the 3rd (Special Reserve) Battalion. This Battalion was based at Fort George, Inverness and so, for the first time in his career, Teddy would be stationed in the Highlands of Scotland.

Documentary evidence is fragmentary, but it seems that Teddy was appointed to help with the reestablishment of the 3rd ('Reserve') Battalion Seaforth Highlanders which was created in 1908. The original 3rd Battalion having been disbanded in 1901 on their return from serving in Egypt, where Teddy would undoubtedly have known them well. This was part of a national reorganisation of the Volunteers and Militia in 1908, with the Volunteers becoming the Territorial Force and the Militia the Special Reserve. As a highly experienced

---

[61] That didn't mean his affinity with horses was over though, and even as late as April 1914 he is recorded as winning a regimental point to point race at Shorncliffe aboard his horse Snipe - Broad Arrow - 17 April 1914

regular solider by this point, it would have made a lot of sense for Teddy to train the Reservists.

He was frequently a judge at regimental boxing matches, but also had time to dedicate to golf while based at Fort George in Inverness. Within a year, he was nominated as Captain of the Ardersier Golf Club at Fort George and on 10 July 1909 he opened the Ardersier Golf Club House. Perhaps golf filled the void left by polo.

Teddy continued to wield a cricket bat to great effect and his arrival at Fort George was marked by the Northern Scot and Moray & Nairn Express[62] who trumpeted:

> *Captain Campion who has played first class cricket in England is a good bat and a "googley" bowler*

While in Scotland, he played cricket regularly, not just for the Seaforths, but also for the North of Scotland.

While all this sport must have been enjoyable, he was not insensitive to the fact that his career had somewhat stalled. In part, it was because the relatively long period of peace had meant there was little action, which meant less chance of promotion. But one can sense that he also feels he is not being taken seriously and he writes movingly to his old Commanding Officer Granville Egerton on his promotion to Colonel in July 1909:

---

[62] 15 May 1909

> *Alas & alack I fear such a future is not for me, I learned too late the "importance of being earnest", and 'tis hard work to live down one's past; in fact I doubt it can be done.*

His time at Fort George was largely spent working with and training the 3rd Battalion and there is an account of the 3rd Battalion's annual inspection in 1909 in which Teddy would have been heavily involved:

> *The Battalion attended 21 days of training at the Common at Fort George under canvas from 6th to the 26 April 1909 and was commanded by Lieut. Col E.W Horne….At the conclusion of the Annual Inspection which took place on the 16 April the Inspecting Officer caused the following to be published in the Battalion Orders "The Inspecting Officer desires to inform all ranks that he was very much pleased with the appearance of the Battalion today. He considers that both the close order drill and manoeuvre were exceedingly well done and that the high state of efficiency reflects the greatest credit on all concerned. He was especially struck with the fine appearance of the Battalion on parade and the soldierly bearing of the men."*[63]

Teddy was also involved in the regular recruitment drives that were needed to keep a steady flow of men into the reserves. In a letter[64] to Egerton in 1911,

---

[63] Historical Record of the 3rd Battalion Seaforth Highlanders – open shelf, National War Museum

he complains about the difficulty in finding men, with emigration and depopulation of the Highlands clearly now being an issue:

> *Canada sucks Scotland's youth like pap from her mother's breasts. There is nothing to be done, Recruiting up here is a losing game and it will have to be reorganised – worse luck. Still what we've got is better than any other Highland Regiment has, but they are not our concern I have to admit.*

In his role, Teddy encountered a good deal of regimental politics, something which he clearly disliked, and he regularly expressed his frustration to Egerton. Nonetheless, there were compensations, and while he was in Scotland, he found time for some of the glittering events of the Highland Season, including attending the Lochaber Gathering and the Northern Meeting Balls in both 1909 and 1910, dancing the night away with the cream of British Society.

There is only one more mention of Teddy's time in Scotland, when in June 1911 the 3rd Seaforths were doing their musketry training and the best shooting company was C Company, commanded by Teddy[65]. But he was to leave Fort George and the 3rd Battalion in January 1912 when, with the prospect of war on the horizon, Teddy transferred back to the 2nd Battalion of the Seaforths at their barracks at Shorncliffe in Sussex. He would stay with the 2nd Battalion for the remainder of his career.

---

[64] Egerton Archive - M.1994.112.35 - March 17th 1911
[65] Northern Chronicle and General Advertiser for the North of Scotland - 03 May 1911

With cricket never far from his mind[66], Teddy immediately reappears on the 2nd Battalion's cricket team, playing consistently against opposition at their Shorncliffe base near Folkestone. As improbable as it now seems, these matches continued right up to the outbreak of war in 1914, with matches against the Field Artillery in June, where Teddy got 115 runs[67]. Later that month, the team played against the Royal Warwickshire Regiment, beating them by over 100 runs; Teddy scored 60 not out and was described as "batting splendidly"[68]. In July, against the Lancashire Fusiliers, he scored 99 before being caught out. His last pre-war match was on the 1 August 1914 against the Royal Marines, where he scored a more modest 17 runs before being bowled out.

All in all, Teddy had an impressive sporting record over nearly two decades. Had he survived the war, one can imagine that he would have continued to play for many years; it was clearly a sport that he loved.

But war in Europe was now imminent, and a mere three weeks after that last cricket match, Teddy would be propelled into the most intense and deadly conflict of his military career, a conflict that would ultimately cost him his life along with so many of his contemporaries.

---

[66] More cerebral pursuits were possible too, and he came second in a national essay writing competition in 1912, although what the topic was we are none the wiser!
[67] Folkestone, Hythe, Sandgate & Cheriton Herald, 06 June 1914
[68] Folkestone, Hythe, Sandgate & Cheriton Herald, 13 June 1914

From the Frontline of History

Officers of the 1st Battalion Seaforth Highlanders at the Kasr El-Nil Barracks Cairo 1902, Teddy front row second left

(Highlanders Museum)

1st Battalion Seaforth Officers on manoeuvres, Sailana, Rajputana, 1905

Teddy front row, second on left

(Private Collection)

From the Frontline of History

Winners of Infantry Cup, 1904, Meerut

From left Capt. C.A. Carden, Lieut K.G. Buchanan, 2nd Lieut. K.D.M. MacLachlan, Capt. E Campion, Front seated unknown

(Private Collection)

From the Frontline of History

Winners of the Rajputana and Central India Polo Cup, 1904

2nd Lieut. K.D.M. MacLachlan, Capt. C.A. Carden, Mr Laverton, Capt. E. Campion

Image courtesy of Lyon & Turnbull Fine Auctioneers

From the Frontline of History

1st Battalion Inter-Company Tug of War won by D Company, 1904,

Teddy seated middle row second left

(Private Collection)

From the Frontline of History

Teddy, taken in Folkestone, presumably when he was stationed at Shorncliffe just before World War One

(Private Collection)

Chapter 9 Teddy and the Great War

It is easy to think that Teddy existed in a dreamy bubble in those leisurely pre-war years, an endless summer of cricket and hunting. He writes in an undated letter to his Aunt Shay[69]:

> ….You've asked me for the very few days I think I can get away: On Thursday Aug 6 I think I can present myself at Rye ready to try and play golf at any rate for three days. And I shall love it. Wish you could have come to the Regiment Games, my company won easily and carried one in a most uncomfortable and hazardous position on their shoulders in a chair to their rooms: it cost me 17/6 in bar – very expensive ride. Also I ran the tea and the strawberry messes were equal to Rolands[70]. Cannot get up to Varsity match or Eton vs Harrow. I wish I could, but work and cricket prevents. Have attained 500 runs this season, not bad for an old man of 40 6/12ths…

In reality, he and the rest of the professional army knew what was coming, and he had been helping to prepare the Regiment for several years before war was actually declared on 4 August 1914. Teddy had been with the 2nd Battalion since 1912 and was under no illusions. He writes in another (undated) letter to his Aunt Shay:

---

[69] Charlotte Susan Seymour, married to his uncle Charles Walter Campion
[70] The Eton common room / restaurant

From the Frontline of History

I am at present in command of 540 men waiting to shoot Germans! If there is war, we shall probably return to Shorncliffe at an early date and be held in readiness to proceed to the continent. We expected to mobilise Friday evening and every minute that we don't is an added chance of peace, but it seems hopeless to restrain these foreign governments from rushing into war and I really think they had better do it and get it over, silly excitable asses who know not what war means!

As is often the way, the professional soldiers are more wary than the politicians about rushing into a conflict although there is a sense that he, like so many, thought it would be over quickly. The British Army at this stage of the war was relatively small at around 250,000 men, half of whom were stationed around the Empire. This hard core of professional soldiers was supplemented by around 270,000 reservists and additional reserves – like the 3rd Battalion of the Seaforths that Teddy had spent so many years training. These were the troops that would be deployed in the early, bloody battles of the war and who would be annihilated as the war progressed. By contrast, the army of the British Empire at the end of the First World War in 1918 numbered over 3.8 million.

As had already been shown during the Boer War, the British Army had outdated notions of modern warfare which had been thoroughly overturned by the Boer conflict. In World War One, the Germans would again teach them the error of trying to fight the current war in the same way as the previous one. This was no colonial war, where the might and technological superiority of the

British Empire could swiftly overcome all opposition, however brave. In the First World War Britain faced a modern and technologically equal power, if not indeed a superior one and, despite the bravery and experience of the British Expeditionary Force that was sent to confront the Germans in 1914, they were on the back foot from the start.

The 2nd Battalion Seaforth Highlanders were mobilised on 4 August 1914 – the very day that war was declared. By 7 August they had already been joined by 620 reservists. They then entrained from Shorncliffe to York and spent the next week moving around the country before being embarking for France from Southampton on 22 August onboard the *SS Lake Michigan*, landing in Boulogne on 23 August and that night entraining to join the 10th Infantry Brigade and be pitched straight into the Battle of Le Cateau.

The British Expeditionary Force first encountered the German Army on 22 August, and on 23 August were hotly engaged in the Battle of Mons as they tried to slow the German attempt to turn the allied flank[71] and allow the French time to retire after their defeat at the Battle of Charleroi. The German offensive was too strong though, however, and the British had to retire. The Battle of Le Cateau was the first action in a two week long retreat that would take the Seaforths practically to the gates of Paris.

Teddy wrote an account of this retreat that is gripping in its description of the ferocious force that the Seaforths faced and the tremendous distances they

---

[71] The Schlieffen Plan

had to cover. This could not have been more different from the pitched battles of Sudan or the skirmishing of the Boer Commandos. The account is so extraordinary that it is repeated verbatim in Colonel John Sym's History of the Seaforth Highlanders[72] and is worth repeating here in its entirety:

The Retreat from Le Cateu: 24 August – 5 September 1914

> On Monday, 24th August, we reached Le Cateau at 3 p.m., and had a very hot march to Beaumont. It became evident that the pace was going to try our Reservists severely. Beaumont seemed extremely peaceful although we knew heavy fighting was going on not very far away.
>
> We left Beaumont at 2 a.m. on 25th August, and knew we were to cover a retirement of some sort, probably we thought of some trenches we had seen the Camerons digging near Le Cateau.
>
> At 6 a.m., just short of a place called St. Python, we halted and had our breakfast (bully beef, bread and jam), and here we first heard the sound of War; at first Artillery fire, but shortly afterwards the rattle of musketry away on our left flank. The noise was no new one to several of us who had seen Service, but none of us before had been pitch-forked from the safety, the comfort, the peace of England in a few short days into War; even a few hours ago at Beaumont all seemed peaceful and

---

[72] Gale & Polden Ltd 1962

quiet and just like any town might appear when full of Troops on manoeuvres. It was a beautiful summer morning; the landscape, large, open and rolling, the crops, cut and standing in stooks, seemed to ask why no one came to harvest them, and away out there, out of sight, came the sound of nations in anger, the deep mutter of guns, and the sharp rattle of rifles.

I was sent off to the right flank to observe, but though getting a splendid view over St. Olesmes, could see nothing, and rejoined the Brigade, which had retired to a farm near Viesly, where B and D Companies entrenched, while A (my Company) and C went about a mile further back, and strengthened a very strong position.

We moved back to the farm at about 3.30 p.m. and had tea in a thunderstorm, getting some shelter for the men in a large barn. At 4.30 p.m. firing became much closer, and we hurried the men out of the barn, and back behind the buildings in Reserve, only getting out just in time before the Germans opened with Artillery (field guns). They gave Baillie's Company a pretty good doing, their fire being very accurate, but several shells failed to burst; the enemy then proceeded to fire over the farm at where they thought the Reserve was; they were about right, as they very nearly got us, causing us to move the men a little further back, and separate the Platoons. The first shell or two astonished the men a good deal, but they were very quiet and steady. The evening early grew dark and rainy, which put an end to this small action.

From the Frontline of History

We now heard that some of our troops had got into trouble in St. Olesmes, which necessitated our staying where we were while another Brigade went to their help. We put out outposts, and at about 9 p.m. there was a burst of firing at an Uhlan patrol who came clattering up the pave taking no precautions whatever—result, one Uhlan and a horse. At 11 p.m. we retired, having had some half-a-dozen casualties and the Commanding Officer's horse wounded.

I shall never forget that march, we had not grown accustomed to the sights and sounds of war, which at the commencement of a campaign impress themselves very acutely on the memory. All around our right flank were burning villages; thoughts and imagination were easily stirred. What had been going on around them? Fierce fighting undoubtedly, the scream of shell, the swish of bullets, steel meeting steel.

We marched all night, passing through Ligny in the early hours of the morning, and reaching Hancourt about 3 a.m. on 26th August, where, in a field we (tired out and short of sleep) threw ourselves down in stooks, and were soon snoring.

At daylight we were making arrangements for breakfast when a furious machine-gun fire opened on two Regiments of our Brigade who were close by. Apparently all night we must have been moving in close proximity to the enemy; probably we thought we were covered by our Cavalry, but in any case we were rudely taught the lesson of not having adequate local protection. I don't think, at the end of this night march, anyone quite knew where anyone else was; It was probably due to neglect of proper co-operation between Brigades, in any case the Brigades were without outposts. The casualties in those Regiments that came under this fire were heavy, and of course effected in a few minutes.

I fancy this must have been a very anxious moment for the Divisional General; there were two obvious positions that could be taken up, one of which was nearer the enemy than the other and for which we should probably have had to fight. The other, the position we retired to, meant a retrograde movement in the face of the enemy. The Germans had not got up their Artillery and Infantry and so we just had time to back and make shelter trenches, mere rabbit scratches, before the serious business of the day.

We were particularly careful to mask our small trenches (cutting the sods ready to place them on the parapet directly the enemy showed) and to this I am sure was due the very few casualties that occurred, although shells were bursting short and over us all day.

The engagement was entirely an Artillery one, the firing from both sides being fast and furious; the Germans were in a numerical superiority of some four guns to one. We had a battery some 300 yards straight behind us, one some 400 yards in front, and another 600 yards to our right rear, so were able to see the effect of the enemy's fire very well. Our fire seemed certainly the more accurate, indeed during the whole morning there were very few German shells that seemed dangerous. They fired mostly shrapnel with a few explosive ones. We fired entirely shrapnel.

About 12 noon the fire became very severe, and we had been made uncomfortable by two premature bursts from the Battery behind us, in addition to having a fair number of badly directed German shells, some bursting just short and some just over.

After this there was a lull until the afternoon, when the enemy appeared to have moved further to our right, which I always have believed to have been a grave mistake, as our left was dangerously in the air. However, their fire became even heavier, and certainly straighter—the Battery behind began to lose; shells were pitching among the guns to our right rear, and the Battery in front looked in a dangerous position, shells bursting across their route of retirement (they did get away later on, though with some loss). We had so far never moved, but the Dover Brigade made an attack to recover their wounded, and the Irish Fusiliers, Warwickshires, and Dublin Fusiliers moved out towards Hancourt, where I believe, they had a certain amount of fighting.

About 4 p.m. a body of our Cavalry moved up on our left, and were engaged by German Infantry, who moved to the attack very rapidly, but across our front at 3,000 yards; they got badly knocked about, being taken in enfilade by our guns.

At about 5 p.m. the German guns put forward a great effort, and their fire was terrific; the sight was magnificent, everywhere on the horizon were our shells bursting and all around, right, left, and near us, theirs did the same; our Gunners were splendid and although heavily outnumbered, fought in a most gallant manner.

At a little after 6 p.m. we got the order to retire from the left, which left me the last Company. The Germans, of course, had the range to a nicety, and gave us a pretty doing over the 400 yards we had to go, my Company losing 17 Men in a few minutes.

We then did Rearguard for about 2 miles, until ordered to close, where the Battalion (minus Baillie's Company which had retired with the Division), and 300 men of the Irish Fusiliers, were to spend the night.

It was a cold miserable, rainy night; our Transport and horses had gone on, so we just laid down where we were, with the Outposts out, and tried to sleep. Our wounded—some 25—were put into a farm, for we had no ambulances. No one understood what the game was, though we supposed we were Rearguard to the Division, but no one knew where the Division was.

Before dawn, on 27th August, the General, who by then, I think, realised that we were isolated, moved us, preparatory to moving off towards the Division directly it was light enough to see. We were certainly in a strange and precarious position 6 miles from our nearest friends and in close proximity to the Germans.

At the first glimmer of dawn one of the enemy's motor cars glided silently along a road some 400 yards off; would they see us? Had they machine guns, and would they stop and fire? We were in close order and dared not move. It dipped over the hill and out of sight, and we prayed we had not been spotted

Then we set off to leg it as fast as possible to rejoin the Division, which we did that afternoon, and were welcomed by the General, who had given us up for lost!

It had been a very trying march; we were foodless; it got hot, and there was no time to get our greatcoats off, still less to get the men water, and they suffered a deal with thirst. My breakfast consisted of a slice of swede, two plums, a small piece of bread, and a most delicious baked potato, given me by a dear old French woman. My feet were very bad, as also were most of the men's, due a great deal to having got them wet through walking in root fields during the Rearguard the previous evening.

We now got the men a few biscuits and then offed it again till evening; a sorely bedraggled battalion, and most unlike the one that had swung down the streets of Boulogne whistling the Marseillaise only four days ago.

Even now we were only accorded a short rest before setting off to march all night. Many of the men by now were quite unable to walk further, and were put on gun carriages and country carts; fortunately my pony turned up, and I sat on him, although, poor beast, he was very sick and tired. It was a dreadful night, the kaleidoscopic effect of figures moving on a road at night when you are dog-tired makes you see all sorts of pictures in the sky, you violently shake your head and pinch yourself, only to wake for a moment and then doze off again; want of sleep becomes real pain.

At 4 a.m. on 28th August we tumbled into a farm; I just glanced in to see that my Company were all right, and then, throwing myself into the straw, knew nothing till 7 a.m., when we breakfasted. We trekked all day, starting directly after breakfast. We were Rearguard moving mostly across country, and arrived at Bussy at 5.30 p.m.

On this day we lost all our kits; I believe the cart carrying them got in the way, and not being able to get out of it quick enough, they were all pitched off and burned.

On Saturday, 29th August, Baillie's Company and mine were sent out on Outpost duty, and during the day watched our Cavalry and Horse Artillery keeping the enemy at arm's length; they retired in the afternoon, and the Germans shelled ground to our right in a somewhat desultory fashion. On my right was a village, Crissolles, held by a Battalion belonging to a Brigade not in our Division. Late in the afternoon, whilst making dispositions for the night, I found this Battalion about to move, which left us entirely in the air. Hastily throwing a Platoon into the village, I galloped off to inform our Brigadier, who moved up a Company to strengthen our line and to hold the village. Here is an example of bad co-operation—one Brigadier moving his Brigade without informing the Brigadier on his left; a Battalion moving without letting the neighbouring troops know. The enemy were in the near proximity; had they attacked our right we should have been in a pretty mess, and to this sort of thing we owe the greater part of the casualties suffered during the Retreat.

In the afternoon of this day we were treated to a novel and most exciting episode; an air fight; a German biplane being attacked by a French monoplane. The latter was a deal the faster, and played the part of the hawk to perfection, swooping up above its enemy, diving towards it, whilst both combatants fired with revolvers—it was quite thrilling, the fight going on until both planes were eventually lost to view.

At 9 p.m. we were ordered to rejoin the Battalion, and the Brigade marched most of that night.

On Sunday, 30th August, we had a very long march with no food, through Noyon to Genancourt, where we had a good night's rest.

31st August—Rather pretty and long march through the forest of Compiegne; a good halt half-way enabled us to have a nice picnic lunch, the men cooking up bully, etc. There were bodies of Uhlans in the wood, but they did not come near us except on one occasion, when Corporal Watson had a shot and missed!

Tuesday, 1st September—Sedan Day! It began badly for us, a Cavalry Regiment and a Battery being badly taken on at dawn by German guns, which had been allowed to entrench within 400 yards. The Battery lost a lot of men and horses, but reorganised, and with their rifles attacked and, helped by Cavalry and Middlesex Regiment, captured several German guns and a lot of prisoners. We took up a couple of Rearguard positions, but were not attacked. This had been another day without food, and I fancy we were lucky to get any, as our Supply Column was very nearly captured by the enemy's Cavalry, who were that evening close to the village of Baron, where we spent the night.

On 2nd September we started very early, my Company escorting Field Ambulances. The Brigade-Major was present seeing us start off, and looked quite worn out, being unable to keep his eyes open for more than a few minutes at a time. A peaceful day—got into Dammartin in time for lunch.

From the Frontline of History

On outposts all night; at 8.30 p.m. a fusillade in front of one of my Picquets, which turned out to be some of our Cyclist Company shooting at the North Irish Horse and wounding three men.

The next day a long march to Bois De Chigny where we had a real night's rest, not getting up till 6 a.m. on 4th September, and rested all day till 5 p.m., when we moved to Serris. I had now entirely run out of cigarettes and matches, both being unobtainable in France at this period of the War.

On 5th September we moved off at 3.30 a.m., and reached Chevry at 12 noon, where we found any amount of vegetables, and after a good wash in the afternoon we had an excellent dinner.

That was the end of the Retreat.

As far as we were concerned it was difficult always to know what we were up to; we were ignorant of the reason of this retirement, although it was daily evident that the enemy were in superior force; always we felt doubtful of our left flank.

Before War began we all realised that our weakness lay in the number of Reservists who would join us; we knew they would be unfit, have forgotten discipline, would not know their Officers, nor they them, and in this weakness lay the difficulty of the Retreat. The other difficulties are manifest ones, but none easy to overcome. Ignorance of what we were doing, hunger at times, thirst at times, but chiefly the fatigue of *long marches on the very barest modicum of sleep. I do not believe the Force ever lost morale, though at times they were almost too tired to fight.*[73]

German Advance (Schlieffen Plan)

14th Aug Shorncliffe
Dover
Calais
Dunkirk
Ypres
Boulogne 23rd Aug
Lille
Arras
Dieppe
Mons
Viesly 25th Aug
St Python
Le Cateau 24th Aug
Hancourt (26th Aug)
St Quentin
Crissoles (29th Aug)
Noyons (30th Aug)
Bussy
Genancourt
Foret de Compiegne (31 Aug)
Verbier
Baron (1st Sep)
Reims
Bois de Chigny (4th Sep)
Paris

Seaforth Highlanders' Route to War
August 1914

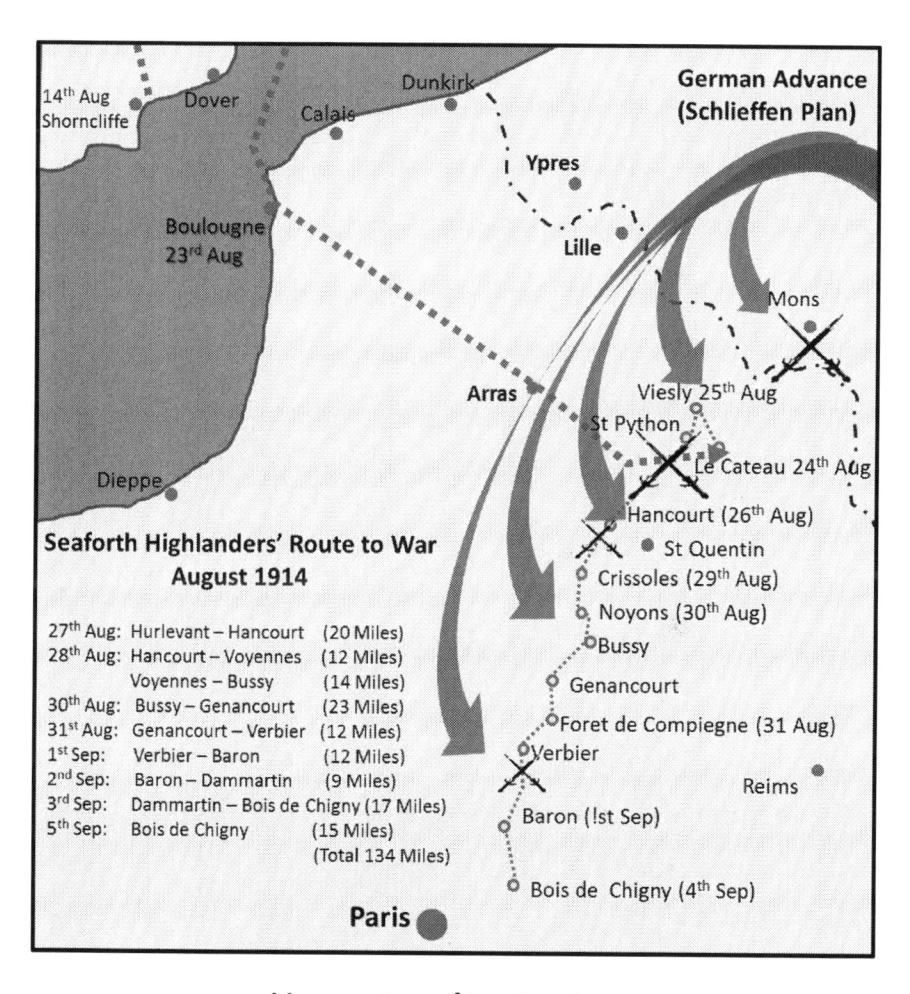

27th Aug:	Hurlevant – Hancourt	(20 Miles)
28th Aug:	Hancourt – Voyennes	(12 Miles)
	Voyennes – Bussy	(14 Miles)
30th Aug:	Bussy – Genancourt	(23 Miles)
31st Aug:	Genancourt – Verbier	(12 Miles)
1st Sep:	Verbier – Baron	(12 Miles)
2nd Sep:	Baron – Dammartin	(9 Miles)
3rd Sep:	Dammartin – Bois de Chigny	(17 Miles)
5th Sep:	Bois de Chigny	(15 Miles)
	(Total 134 Miles)	

Map courtesy of Lee Smart

---

[73] "The Battalion since 8pm on the 25th August have marched 155 miles (11 days) and during this period spent one day (26th) in action and 1 day (4th) in resting and refitting." 2nd Battalion Seaforth Highlanders War Diary, Aug – Dec 1914

From the Frontline of History

Chapter 10 The Marne and Aisne

The Battles of Mons and Le Cateau and the subsequent retreat shattered any illusions that the British might have had over the superiority of their forces. Of the 40,000 British servicemen that fought at Le Cateau there were over 7,800 casualties[74] and the Seaforths ended the retreat at Bois de Chigny, less than 25 miles from Paris. In their opening attack of the war, the Germans had come within touching distance of the French capital. The British, who for over a decade had enjoyed relative peace, had received the rudest of awakenings. The War was only two weeks old and the Seaforths, one of its most experienced battalions, were already shattered and exhausted. But it was going to get a lot worse.

Over the next few days, the Seaforths marched as rapidly as possible due east from Paris to try and stop the Germans crossing the river Marne at La Ferté. On 9 September, the Brigade were waiting for the crossing of the River Marne to be effected by the 11th and 12th Brigades. This was prevented by the enemy's machine guns which were positioned in a house and proved very difficult to dislodge or locate for the artillery. The Brigade finally crossed the Marne by using a railway bridge near Sausson Chateau, three miles north east

---

[74] Edmonds, J. E. (1926). Military Operations France and Belgium, 1914: Mons, the Retreat to the Seine, the Marne and the Aisne August–October 1914. History of the Great War Based on Official Documents by Direction of the Historical Section of the Committee of Imperial Defence. II (2nd ed.). London: Macmillan

of La Ferté. Over the next few days, in conjunction with the French, they helped push the Germans back.

On 14 September, early in the morning, the Seaforths reached La Montagne Farm, North of Bucy-Le-Long and took up their position sandwiched between the Rifle Brigade on their right and the Hampshire Regiment on their left. Teddy was commanding A Company, which was one of two companies put into the firing line, digging in as best they could after a hurried reconnaissance. The first Battle of the Aisne had begun.

As soon as it was light, intermittent artillery fire opened up, raining down shells on their position. At about 9 a.m., disaster struck when the Seaforths lost their Commanding Officer, Lt-Col Sir Evelyn Bradford, who was killed instantly by a shrapnel shell. He had been reconnoitring the enemy's position together with the Commanding Officer of the Rifle Brigade when he was hit. It was a major loss so early in the conflict. Captain Stockwell assumed command, with Teddy becoming the Acting Senior Major, the second in command of the Battalion, relinquishing command of A Company.

German artillery continued to pound them while the German trenches raked their position with machine gun fire. The heavy level of fire suggested that an infantry attack was imminent and the frontline was reinforced with B and C Companies and a detachment of Gordon Highlanders, but ultimately no attack came. The intermittent shelling continued through the day and was a major cause of casualties as it prevented them from entrenching their position properly.

From the Frontline of History

On that first day of the battle, the Seaforths alone had lost their Commanding Officer, and one other officer, and had one other officer wounded, eight NCOs and men killed or mortally wounded, and another 58 wounded. Their fellow Highlanders – the Gordons – had suffered 18 casualties.

During the night and early morning, the Seaforths adapted their position, using respite from the shell fire to dig trenches behind the crest of the hill so that they were invisible to the enemy. A Company's supports were placed in a cave that lay between a sunken road and the trenches which were on a rounded hilltop about 400 yards apart. The cave would become a valuable refuge from the shell fire over the days ahead. Teddy's company was relieved under cover of darkness, and after more than 24 hours on the firing line he must have been glad to get some rest.

Shell fire continued to catch any unwary men that were out in the open, but most of the troops were better protected now they were entrenched and the shrapnel was less dangerous than before. The next few days were quieter, and Teddy had a chance to write to General Granville Egerton on 17 September[75] describing the death of Bradford and his thoughts on his first three weeks of the war:

> *You will have heard about the Colonel, much bad luck, he was simply first class out here as indeed he was everywhere – he always knew his mind, made it up instantly and instantly acted on it by a kind of roster*

---

[75] National War Museum, Egerton Archive - M.1994.112.24

he kept in his head each day whatever came to hand to be done came to the team of Companies and officers for that day be selected (except for some very special reason) so all knew they had an equal chance of being 1st in at the enemy. We have pushed across a river on the Sunday/Monday night and an early dawn had to take up a position which we had no time to entrench, he & I went round it in the dark at about 3 a.m. & decided on the position for mine and Anstruther's companies and then we scratched rabbit scrapes and were very heavily shelled all day – I was with my Coy and didn't know till noon of his death which occurred while he was talking to Biddulph from the [Rifle Brigade] over some situation. He was killed instantly and was laid to rest in a lovely spot overlooking a beautiful valley. We have had a wooden cross put up and we are still in the same position as on Monday – I almost feel his gallant spirit must be watching & helping us[76].

This is a weird war – we know nothing really of what is going on and have just to do the job we are asked to do as well as we can and the men are excellent – very long marches and being shelled without hitting back; their marching could have been better but their coolness under fire is admirable and at night they are not excitable ...

....These Germans are damn good in most ways and we shall have lots of trouble with them unless movements from Belgium and Russia checkmates 'em into chucking it: I fancy their infantry do not like

---

[76] Underlined in blue pencil

> attacking ours any more, but their artillery can shoot jolly well and are most bloody unpleasant. Their prisoners are rather [dour], are all looking well fed and in good condition; whatever our papers say I suspect they get plenty of rations & that their staff work is excellent.

Not for the first time, Teddy criticises the attitude of the newspapers which tried to downplay the strength of the German forces – he could see that the reality on the ground was very different.

The weather now deteriorated, and it became very cold, with heavy rain and even hail. The troops were uncomfortable as very few had both greatcoats and waterproof sheets, so they would either be dry or warm, but not both. One disadvantage of the greatcoats was that once they were wet, they took a very long time to dry out and became incredibly heavy.

Teddy picks up the narrative in a typed manuscript from 21 September[77]. Given all the military detail, it was most probably written to his brother Bill, who was then commanding the Royal Sussex Regiment:

> *My last ended our first days fighting north of the Aisne and here we are still, having been here a week. It is a curious life, imagine any wooded hillside; below it is a valley some two miles wide rising to hills with spurs and narrow valleys, all wooded, and beyond on either side the high bare uplands with in the distance a row of poplar trees marking the line of some high road in the valley of the Aisne itself, cuddling softly*

---

[77] Danny Archive: ACC/5653/2/15

against the bottom of the hills, little grey French villages with their brown tiled roofs and the sharp straight lines of their church spires; and then, on the valley side of our own hill imagine the whole ground terraced with small caves and you might well ask – "why have a lot of idiots made such a mess?"

Had you lived here during this last week you would not have wondered why, for like a lot of ants have men, armed with pick and spade, sought the shelter of Mother Earth against a nasty, buzzing, tearing, destructive enemy, whose whole aim is to destroy all those who refuse to seek such shelter.

Under the cover of darkness after our first day's fighting, every hour was used in first of all making such trenches as would adequately protect our men against shell fire. Digging into the hillside so that our supports and reserves might rest secure after their nights of watchfulness in the trenches. Making obstacles away in front, to hold the enemy where we could destroy him, making communications so that food, water, ammunition could be got to the fighting line with a minimum of risk, and we made our defences strong, for our respect of the German artillery is high.

As the week wore on, our little caves have assumed quite a habitable appearance. Straw has been placed at the bottom, covers of boughs give protection against sun and rain, chiefly the latter, and at any time of day man can be seen calmly sleeping, while the shells sing harmlessly by, sometimes high overhead, winging their way to the other side of the valley, sometimes bursting, and whipping the trees with their contents.

We have 'days' of shelling; one day may be quite a peaceful one, another, our foe would seem to be in a temper, and the line of our trenches becomes alive with puffs of bursting shell, This wakes up our own gunners, then both sides proceed to 'go' for each other. After this, the Germans seem to think they will catch our supports and reserves, and search our hillside up and down and along, using up much ammunition in what seems to be a senseless rage. For at these outbursts, we merely smile.

Often their fire is directed by their aeroplanes; and this we hate. The cooperation between the man in the air and the man behind the gun is truly excellent, if a battery gets spotted in this way, it is in for a bad time. For us infantry, the matter is not so serious, we bolt into our 'junk holes'. But guns and transport cannot suddenly vanish into the bowels of the earth.

Thursday last was a particularly bad day. After a lot of ordinary and high explosive shrapnel at our trenches, the enemy began dropping six inch 90lb howitzer shells all about the place. In front of and behind the trenches, and searching the side of our hill. These shells burst on impact and making big holes in the ground, throw up a volume of earth and stones beside making a great noise.

Soon however they went even one better, and we were disturbed by enormous explosions. I am not exaggerating when I say they created local earthquakes. One went into the ground just in front of my cave and literally covered me with falling earth and stuff, then they found the position of a battery nearby. Knocked a lin to pieces and caused the gunners to leave their guns a while.

After this they made merry with a village in which was our transport, also putting one of those monstrous projectiles into a Battalion, considered safe, which did much damage. This jolly instrument of war has been called by our gunners 'Aunt Sally'. It throws a 280lb projectile the base of which is 8.2 inches. I must say these big chaps make me feel a bit nervous, they were wonderfully accurate, and it seemed they might blow us eventually 'bang' off our hill altogether, but against 'personnel' their effect is small. We had three men buried in their cave by one on Friday and we only dug 'em out just in time, but this is the extent of the harm they have done us.

In addition to our trenches and caves, we have a large natural cave in an old stone quarry big enough to hold 200 men and now we have cut steps to enable us to get out quickly. We put most of our men inside, and the officers mess, and sleep here. I am now writing this on a large bed of straw in this big cave and, except for being infernally draughty, it is pretty comfortable.

The weather has been unkind, and trench work at night has really been dreadfully cold, wet and miserable and after bad nights the sun has often refused to warm or dry us during the day. Otherwise though a lazy life, after the hard work we have had it would have been a most pleasant change; we get our mails regularly almost every day, and comforts in the way of cigarettes chocolate are beginning to arrive.

We are, of course, hoping to go on, but with an enemy only 1,200 yards away, one holds or attacks in deference to the plan in our Commander's head, and to that we are glad to trust. We have hardly had any casualties, a man now and then is bound to get hit, and last night we had a few from a small night attack, not a serious affair at all.

On 21st September they continued digging trenches so that the reserves could shelter when standing to arms. Captain D.A. Carden, Teddy's longstanding comrade in arms since the Sudan campaign and fellow polo player, was wounded in the hand by a chance shrapnel shell in the front trench towards evening and there was heavy fighting on their right flank during the night. Over the next few days, the weather improved and there were often relatively quiet days, although there was sniping at night.

Teddy took advantage of these quiet days to write to his family and friends and on 25 September he again wrote to Egerton[78], who was now a General:

---

[78] National War Museum, Egerton Archive - M.1994.112.25

I would have written more often but there is little news to give, also our letters appear to take 14 days or so to get home so all is stale by the time you get them.

Very many thanks for your cuttings, they are much appreciated. I have sent home three letters and told my sister to send them to the editor of the Morning, to try and rake in a shilling or two.

They are, as far as I can remember, quite inoffensive and I do not talk of "stacks of dead" or "sticking squealing Germans" or other lies.

I just wrote a very tame account of our doings from 25th of August to 5th September[79], another about the action here on the 14th of September, and another of life in the trenches. No names mentioned and no regiments.

Good God, the Daily Mail sickened me worse a good deal than soldiers' letters, for the man who writes is supposed to be at least educated. Whatever, he is a consummate liar. These Germans have fallen back in very good order and have held up very [closely] and at one point with very few men (1,000 men and some maxims versus a division of ours).

Very possibly they were tired and disappointed but they have never become demoralised. The French fought very hard and very well and

---

[79] The Retreat from Le Cateau – repeated in full above

especially their Zouaves who are of the bravest. Our troops are doing damn well. One or two lessons we have learned may be of use.

First, if a great many of our casualties and a large amount of the missing had been due to really bad cooperation you would hardly believe me when I assert as facts that on more than one occasion one brigade is retired without informing the brigade on right or left. I think (I will not say for certain) Divisional Commanders have been ignorant of the whereabouts of their neighbouring divisions.

Companies and Battalions have often retired without informing those on their flanks and that is why you hear of people being cut off. One day I was linked up on day [fireposts] with another battalion and ordered to make my dispositions and take up my position for the night. At dusk, the battalion from the other brigade on my right retired without telling me or my General. They left a village on my right unheld. I shooed a platoon in there (it had been held by battalion) and galloped 'ventre à terre' 1½ miles to the G.O.C.

I was damned angry, but this sort of thing is frequent. Then officers do not read their maps carefully enough. If they are suddenly given a job, they go the wrong way. There is not enough importance in every officer who has a map knowing exactly where he is at any time.

Any scratch in the ground is better than nothing, I had half an hour or so to dig on 14th. My men were 15 hours under shellfire, most of it fired short range, and my total casualties (16) were less than during one 10 minute retreat under shellfire on 26th of August.

I fancy no attack, unless ground is extraordinarily favourable, can be pushed home against present day artillery & machine gun fire, one may gain a little and make it good, and that may be chiefly done at night.

I fancy the Germans are nervous at night, and I think that dusk and dawn are the best times to get at 'em. The Germans attack more often at dusk than dawn.

We want crowds of kit, and motor machine guns out here, they would be invaluable. I would love to command 1,000 men on horses with six pom poms on motors and a dozen machine guns.

We are all well and fit. Derrick poor old chap got a nasty smack in the hand three days ago and will now have to go home – Anstruther was wounded on the 14th and Nipper's head is still bad, we got letters from him.

The next day, Teddy wrote again to his brother Bill, sharing some of the insights that he had learned during the course of the fighting[80]:

Dear Bill

---

[80] Danny Archive: ACC 563/2/15

From the Frontline of History

Many thanks for yours. You must come out in Command; you certainly deserve it after so many years of combining soldiering with other strenuous works. I am wondering if a few hints as to the kit would be useful any note. I'll be sure [illegible].

Since 25th August besides a suitable uniform I have gathered a sponge, toothbrush, one piece of soap, a pair of socks, a week ago I got two pairs of socks, a vest and a shirt and a waterproof shirt.

So one can get on with quite a little. One must have a canteen, a knife, fork, spoon, a case containing note paper and envelopes, an air pillow, a flask – a mouthful of brandy when chilled through at night is worth a deal. A torch & refills about every 10 days, a cap comforter, a canvas bucket, a British [warm] and a Burberry, a waterproof hat, a compass, washing things; pair socks. All these can be carried on the person and on the horse. Then in 35lb kit you can get a change of clothes – sleeping bag etc.

We lost the whole of our 35lb kits, thrown away and burnt on the 28th August by order of a staff officer – damn the fellow. Am writing this you and two 'good morning' shells have just hurried Eric Campbell under cover with his breeches down and the remark "damn the Swine, they caught me *** that time!"

As regards tactical things, we have learnt there is nothing new but neglect over them has cost a lot of casualties in various units:

1. Cooperation – Brigades often are quite ignorant of position of Brigades on right and left and this goes down to the Platoon commander and has resulted in units getting left and losing lots of casualties and missing. One has to watch right and left all the time.
2. Germans will always try [to out] flank
3. Officers in possession of maps must always know exactly where they are. Companies have taken up wrong positions through neglect of map reading.
4. Patrols at night should move off the road but sure enough not to get lost: they can either elude or capture German patrols.
5. Picquets must put at night some obstacle between them and the enemy.
6. When making trenches make enough to take in the supports.
7. March discipline has been far too lax out here – men falling out to get water and truant without orders
8. Discipline – saluting – movements and handling arms gets very slack and bad
9. Dress – Men will put on any damned irregular thing they can unless stopped – French hats! German hats anything!

These are a few of the things one notices.....

Their aeroplanes are very good and if they see a battalion move will soon get a battery on you: especially reserves in close order.

Well we are all jolly fit and are only longing to get on, but 'tis a slow business. We shall want you all out here, we are all length and no depth. Do you remember my first dinner with your company at Hassocks I said I wished the Regular and Territorial army saw more of each other, as in case of war the Territorial would be sure to come and help his Regular comrade on the continent – its come time enough.

One good success would be a great thing.

We'll dish Willy's Swine dogs soon.

Good luck and hurry up

Teddy

Finally, on 28 September, he writes to his younger sister Alice (always known as Elsie), understandably focusing less on military tactics but instead painting a more vivid picture of what day-to-day life was like[81]:

Dear Else,

You're a ripper for looking after Jennie, thank you ever so much. Poor thing — I think soldiers should do without dogs! They are always being left about.

---

[81] Danny Archive: ACC 5653/2/10

Would you tell Charlie[82] to tell his Times Editor that he really should be more careful how he prints soldiers' letters, they are hopeless exaggerations, and out here they rather sicken us.

In fact the whole tone of the British Press has vastly exaggerated the German retreat; they retired and our Armies made them, which was good business, but in excellent order and put up a gallant rear guard action at La Ferte, indeed 1,000 men and machine guns held up a Division for a considerable time.

They are far from being a beaten and we are only just beginning real business. A great many of our losses have been sheer bad luck with a certain amount of bad management thrown in, Regiments getting caught by [Machine] guns in close order, Regiments getting left behind through not watching movements of troops on the flank, but now these great masses of troops are in touch, manoeuvring for position is nearly over. The attack in depth somewhere must soon be made, and I think our side are in a position to make it from more than one place, and if successful, as it <u>must</u> be, the result should be disastrous or nearly so to the Germans.

I'm glad Mother saw Nipper MacLachlan, he got a nasty knock on the head and didn't take enough care of it, and his head is not his strong point, as he got sunstroke very badly in India.

---

[82] Probably Charles Augustus Phillimore, Elsie's husband

This trench life is weird work: we snipe away at Germans at 1,200 yards and they snipe us: then the guns on either side have a get-to: then their guns give us a doing in the trenches: then a bit of high bird shooting at aeroplanes usually done by us officers, it is very dangerous to our friends: our air gun only shoots a projectile that bursts on graze, so we cannot see where our shells go, but the Deutschers fire their field gun and it is extraordinary pretty to see the white bursting and puffs high up against the blue sky, and they are always behind their bird!

Our mess is in a stone quarry that accommodates also some 400 men: a weird and fantastic sight at night, a few candles stuck about and dim shapes of men, and on an alarm they emerge slowly like ants from the earth and out to their appointed places.

We've dug everywhere into this hill — trenches for this, trenches for that – caves on the hillside - every man grovels his place of safety into Mother Earth, and into it he delves when the shells arrive. I am afraid there is little humour to be got, but we are a happy, laughing, chattering family in our quarry and life though the same every day goes quick, what with the getting of your letters, papers, some new kind of food, some rumour, and sleep, blessed sleep, we make up for what we lost and save the daylight - bed at 9pm, up 4am, sleep 2pm -4pm, dinner at 5.30 etc.

Much love to Jimps and Charley,

Your loving boy,

Teddy

On 5 October, after three weeks of fighting, the battalion received orders to hand over their trenches to the French and Teddy was able to leave the Aisne behind – one cannot imagine he regretted it, although he was not to know that the next battle would be even bloodier.

From the Frontline of History

Chapter 11 In Flanders Fields

Over the next week, the Seaforths marched and travelled north to the Belgian border with France. As the eastern combat zone had sunk into the stasis of trench warfare, the German Army had turned north west in the 'race to the sea' to try and turn the allied flank. Countered by the French and the British all the way, the stage was set for the Battle of Ypres, one of the bloodiest battles in world history, that would be fought out over the next three years. The Seaforths knew by now that this war was a very different beast to the colonial campaigns in which they had fought before. The tone of Teddy's correspondence changes as the horror and exhaustion sets in. His next letters are quite a contrast to the cheerful jottings of his youth in Crete.

Arriving at Caëstre on 13 October, the Seaforths were immediately marched out to the east to confront the Germans north of Flêtre:

About 2.30 p.m. they received orders to attack the German position which was said to extend from Fountain Houck opposite their left on a line southwards through Point 62 and Meteren. We can now pick up the story from the Battalion War diary, which describes the frontage of the Division as follows:

- *10th Brigade from Fountain Houck – Point 62*
- *12th Brigade from Pt 62 to Flêtre - Meteren road*
- *11th Brigade in reserve at Flêtre*
- *6th Division was on our right and 2nd Cavalry Division on our left*

The frontage of the brigade was divided as follows:

- *Seaforth Highlanders right on Point 62*
- *Royal Irish Fusiliers left on Fountain Houck*
- *Royal Dublin Fusiliers in reserve in rear of our left flank*
- *Royal Warwickshire Regiment in reserve in rear of our right flank at Planeboom (withdrawn there as we passed through them)*

At 3.15 p.m. the Battalion deployed to attack – C Coy & D Coy forming firing line and supports with A & B Coys forming reserve. The deployment took place about 1500 yards from the enemy's position. The leading Coys threw out a section extended in front of the leading platoon which took up the frontage allotted to the Coy. After advancing some 500 yards they came under fire, still being unable to locate the enemy's trenches. These could not be seen till a ridge about 600 yards from them was reached. We were then subjected to a fairly accurate though not really heavy fire. Owing to the thick weather prevailing, our guns could not be used to any advantage and were now not firing, and the enemy's trenches could not be clearly seen by us.

Some delay occurred here owing to touch not being properly established with 12th Brigade on our right. Captain Baillie (commanding C Coy) organised an assault on the enemy's position in combination with Royal Irish Fusiliers & Essex Regiment (12th Brigade), Major Stockwell having pushed A Coy up into the firing line the position was carried at the point of the bayonet. A very flat open space had to be crossed by the Battalion which caused them several casualties as the enemy's fire was exceedingly accurate. The Germans evacuated their trenches before we got in with the bayonet and as it was now very dark about 5.45 p.m. pursuit across the enclosed country in front of us was impossible. The position won was entrenched and A Coy put out outposts, the remainder of the Battalion bivouacking in the open. Beyond a certain amount of sniping from the direction of Meteren we were not bothered further that night. Very wet and uncomfortable. We captured one German and they left on the ridge about six dead but covered communications by road to their rear would have facilitated their getting wounded and dead away.

Such was the official description of the Battle of Meteren. Teddy gives a more vivid description in his letters. The first was written to his Aunt Shay[83] on 16 October, thanking her for some gifts that she had sent out. He gives a brief overview of the attack drawing on hunting analogies that would have been well known to her:

> ...three days ago we had a topping good attack which ended in a bayonet charge at dusk when the Germans ran and unfortunately hounds had to be stopped - a pity – my hounds want a bit of blood after all our patient actions under shell fire – but I'll send a decent account of this later.

---

[83] Danny Archive: ACC 5653/2/10

The next day he finds time to write to his brother Bill[84] and gives another vivid description of the bayonet charge:

> *Our men are in great form and were delighted at their performance four days ago – they have fairly smelt blood now and were very determined. We lost just short of 100 – not many considering the swineherds were in trenches. It was glorious – you would have loved it. Just like a wild wonderful 15 minutes over a [illegible] country on the best of horses and no time to look: in fact better. I thrill all over with the thought of it – like that there is no doubt out comes the brute in one and one loves it!*

And on 29 October, writing to an unnamed recipient[85] he goes into further detail:

> *On the 13th October our brigade were Advanced Guard and came up against an enemy who were holding what was evidently a lightly entrenched position; we were ordered to attack, three regiments being allotted a certain frontage, while one was held in reserve. The ground over which we had to advance sloped gently down to a stream and as gently up again to the enemy's position only some 1,000 yards away. They apparently had no artillery, we had, so the job should have been easy, but the afternoon was dark and misty to such an extent that our guns could scarcely help us at all. Indeed, the light was so bad that at*

---

[84] Danny Archive: ACC 5653/2/15
[85] Danny Archive: ACC 5653/2/15

500 yards it was extremely difficult to see the enemy's trenches and almost hopeless to cause him real loss by fire. The result was a carefully planned advance which at 250 yards from our foe dissolved into a wild hooroosh and charge. It was all very exciting and splendid, the men cheered lustily and found yelling a fine method of overcoming fear and laid tongue to all the 'hound language' I could think of.

The enemy bolted at the last moment but unfortunately it had got so dark we could neither pursue nor shoot him and there was nothing to do but have a look at the small 'bag' that remained on the field.

This was our first attack pushed home and the dead victims proved objects of some interest indeed it may be somewhat gruesome to relate, that the men showed much the same gleeful curiosity as is displayed by a small boy inspecting a dead rabbit the first time he is allowed to accompany his father out shooting.

The mist of the afternoon turned into a cold and miserable rain and the night would have been wretched one, had it not been for the thrill and glow of satisfaction which is the aftermath to successful fighting and lessens temporarily at any rate the sorrow caused by casualties.

It is clear that after months of being shelled and sniped at from a distance, he and his men enjoyed getting to grips with their enemy at the point of a bayonet. It must have been intensely disappointing that, having had the enemy on the run, they were then unable to push home their attack.

Over the next days, the Seaforths, with the Royal Dublin Fusiliers on their right, moved to the east with orders to take the town of Frelinghien. They found that the Germans were in an entrenched position to the south of the town. On 19 October, having been shelled by the enemy, at the suggestion of Captain Baillie, the Seaforths advanced towards half a dozen scattered houses south of the town which had been occupied by snipers and which would give them a position to enfilade the enemy's trenches. The Battalion war diary describes the attack:

> The advance was carried out under supporting fire of our guns. It was necessary to crawl round man by man along the river bank which gave some protection from the enemy's position but could be enfiladed if the enemy still held the houses. Three volunteers went first and found the first house unoccupied. The remainder of the Company followed by degrees and all of the houses were gradually occupied before dark. They were subjected to a certain amount of fire and Captain Baillie was unfortunately wounded. The houses were loopholed and placed in a state of defence and it was found that the German trenches were more or less enfiladed by some of them. It had been intended that A Coy should also follow and occupy some of the houses but it was found that there was not enough room and at night they occupied a trench between C Coy and the left of our original line of trenches and two houses on the left of the main road, preparatory to advancing in the morning.

At 4 a.m. [on the 20th] B & D Coy moved on through A Coy (which was left in reserve) and occupied the houses with C Coy. Loopholes and defences were improved and it was arranged to attack the trenches with artillery and with the Irish Fusiliers who were now between the Battalion and the Royal Dublin Fusiliers.

There was a certain amount of fire directed against us in the houses, but no fire from artillery. However, till supported by them we could not advance.

Irish Fusiliers commenced their advance across the open but found it heavily entangled with barbed wire. After a time the enemy's fire slackened under our artillery and it was thought that they had evacuated their trenches. Royal Irish Fusiliers were now advancing towards the German trenches under partial cover of a low bank and thin line of trees and we were preparing to advance into their trenches on our left. A heavy fire was suddenly opened by the enemy who had been lying low in their trenches near us, though most of the line had been evacuated.

We were at that point within 200 yards of them and it was decided to take the position by assault. This was effected at about 11 a.m. by B Coy under a heavy fire, most gallantly led by Captain D.G. Methven & 2nd Lieut J.F. Glass. The latter was wounded attempting to storm the trench, while the former was unfortunately killed shortly after it was taken.

As the trench was on a high steep bank and the ground was very slippery our men had very great difficulty in getting into the trench. They were also brought under crossfire from snipers in a large Brewery on the edge of town near the river.

None of the Germans escaped out of this section of the trench, about 30 being killed and 20 being captured. This trench was now occupied by B Company who advanced and occupied with a few men the edge of the town East of the main road, the Brewery west of the road still being occupied by snipers.

About 1 p.m. several Germans showed the white flag (about 15 men) and leaving their trenches without arms surrendered. Soon after a few more surrendered from some houses in the town. One of these returned to the brewery and brought in three more Germans by arrangement with the Commanding Officer. He also reported that the Brewery was now unoccupied which subsequently proved quite correct. This was about 3.30 p.m.

After dark the Brewery was occupied by 2 ½ platoons of A Coy after a thorough search of the buildings and cellars had been made. The remaining 1 ½ platoons of A Coy occupied houses East of the road with 1 platoon of D Coy. C & D Coys occupied the original houses taken the previous night with headquarters. B Coy occupied the captured trenches with Royal Irish Fusiliers on their right. The position generally was entrenched and placed in a state of defence.

From the Frontline of History

In Teddy's letter of 29 October[86], he describes the same scene:

> ..... we were ordered to clear away the enemy from some houses and to advance as far as we could into the village in front. This proved a very slow business and entailed skilful leading and careful co-operation of artillery and Maxim gun fire. House after house was occupied and loopholed until we were held up by the enemy in some very strongly made trenches on our right flank.
>
> Being in reserve I watched the assault on these in the most intense excitement. Our men worked their way up under the bank to within a few yards of the enemy. The bank was steep and a nasty obstacle, for the moment a man put his head over the top he was within a yard of the muzzle of the enemy's rifles and it was difficult to rush up with any speed. As a spectator it was all one could do not to shout encouragement. However, they needed little, for, led by two gallant officers who both fell, one killed and one wounded in three places, our men soon rushed over the banks and shot the few Germans who bolted; not a man escaped.
>
> They were then led forward by another officer to the occupation of more houses and he also fell mortally wounded, splendidly leading his men against an enemy who concealed and entrenched would have

---

[86] Danny Archive: ACC 5653/2/15

defied the advance of any troops who were not brave men and commanded by brave officers.

During all this attack we were very much helped by a regiment on our right, who manged to enfilade the enemy and between their action and ours the Germans had had about enough and commenced surrendering. All the afternoon we have been much bothered by a large brewery which well loopholed, almost forbade any further advance unless we could have it destroyed by artillery. However, fortunately, the defenders followed the example that had been set them and gave themselves up as prisoners of war. By evening we had gained a good footing in the village and had put what we had won into a state of defence.

The next day it was found quite impossible to venture into any open place whilst the main street was 'commanded' by loopholes manned by snipers, who must have been carefully picked men as their shooting was extremely accurate. The only way to advance was to blow up and bang our way through the middle of houses from one building to another. Late at night we had still three more houses we wanted and just after midnight being practically sure they were unoccupied we proceeded to take them.

I must say it was a nervous business and the worst moment I have had out here was standing in a small yard, pitch dark, thank goodness in company with another officer, when suddenly, without any apparent

From the Frontline of History

reason, through the open door of the house we thought empty came the ringing of an electric bell!......It seems inconceivable that such a thing should have frightened us, but it did and we stood stock still and the beastly bell continued to ring, would it never stop! I don't know what caused this noise but I fancy it was only an alarm clock!

I must have been very jumpy that night for later on I got another shock coming round the corner of a house I knew my men had been into and had reported empty suddenly appeared a light. We were, of course, working without lights of any sort and here was a lamp alight in a house that should be uninhabited for hours. There seemed to be no explanation though we searched the house again from cellar to roof.

Worked on till daylight making loopholes and communications and in my next I will try and tell you of our life in these houses and of where we now are in a trench some 150 yards from our enemy. At such proximity one never knows when one will get time to write, but today things are quiet and I think we have done each other enough harm for a little respite from the usual sniping at which game we are a good deal the better.

The next day he continues the story in a letter dated 30 October[87]:

---

[87] Danny Archive: ACC 5653/2/15

From the Frontline of History

I said I would try and give you some idea of our experiences in the houses, the taking of which I described in my last letter.

First of all, you must understand that every building had been violently bombarded by our own guns firing lyddite shells, and added to the destruction caused by these, we had blown down walls, made loopholes everywhere and generally turned what had been someone's home into a shell of a thing like an old disused sieve.

The Germans had thrown all the clothes, curtains, women's hats, broken china and glass all over the floors and these were thick and deep in with fallen plaster and dust.

The inhabitants all seemed to have kept rabbits, there were also three or four dogs wandering about in an aimless manner, evidently not liking to leave their old homes. There was also a goat and all of them had yellow feet, one rabbit indeed a white one was yellow all over all caused by the explosions of our lyddite.

And now if you could have come with me into a little loft in our most advanced house and moved your head slowly and carefully until through a loophole you could get a view, just down almost at your feet you would have seen a German trench within a stone's throw; the sentry in this room would tell you that he had heard Germans there in the night. A little further off you would see more German trenches extending right away to the East.

Cross the room and with the same care take another peek, opposite, 100 yards away, is a block house and in it you would have been told of a very accurate sniper, who had caused us several casualties. Further to your left, you would have seen some sheds and a loop-holed wall extending down to the river. And now come across the main street, down a ditch we had sapped (for to walk on the road meant a certain pill from our friends in the blockhouse and you would have found yourself in a large brewery almost knocked to pieces, but with a cellar intact and full of beer and a small office we use as a mess.

Again here through loopholes you faced the enemy 150 yards away, also in houses behind loopholed walls. Look up a little and you would see a fine church spire knocked to pieces but still a spire (it is now quite demolished) and look around everywhere and you would see destruction and the results of shell fire, rooms in indescribable confusion, every sort of article lying about in the yards, tossed there by the violent explosion of shells, large beams dangling at impossible and ridiculous angles, large holes torn through them.

Here in these houses we lived for six days and nights a curious life, for a careless movement meant the smack of a bullet always pretty close. We dug trenches and each garden was a regular burrow of pits and small holes for use when the enemy commenced to shell us. Yet we were pretty comfortable, lots of mattresses to sleep on, stoves to cook on, beer from the brewery to drink, but what we hated, and what we had daily to endure, was a regular dose of fire from the enemy's 80lb shells. These were also directed at the Brewery and the men first of all sought shelter in the cellars, afterwards in trenches, but still we had to have men in loopholes to watch for a possible advance of the enemy and these had a thin and anxious time.

We lost comparatively little, although looking on you would have imagined no one could have escaped the explosion of these powerful projectiles. Every sort of thing was sent hurtling through the air, clouds of dust and fragments of brick, wood, bits of shell flew about in all directions and the noise was terrific. Yet at the end of our dose we quietly 'carried on', everyone amazed at the little harm done and curious to see what remained in his own particular little place where he lived and watched. There was always some anxiety as to the beer and we 'cussed' when our well was destroyed.

Monday the 26th of October will always be remembered as 'Portmanteau Day'. It began by the Adjutant reporting that a very large black thing had slowly descended from the sky and fallen through the roof of a shed in the Brewery. The Commanding Officer went to inspect it and found an enormous thing lying harmless but dangerous. Soon after, an explosion; I was the other side of the road and I thought the whole front of the brewery had been blown up and we soon learned the effect of the big black thing that came down from the sky, for you could see them quite plainly, big black things tossed up and as you watched mouth open with astonishment you felt quite certain that the beastly thing was going to come down bang on your own individual head.

The first one bursting somewhere near the Colonel threw him down and when I saw him a few minutes afterwards he was grey and thick with dust and had a cut head.

This last German development was the limit and we had to go or be gradually blown to smithereens. So we slowly retired 200 yards back to the trenches we had taken before. It was rather nervous work, a sort of itching to get away out of the houses and the Brewery, but it all went well.

The Germans must have brought up their siege guns and they had probably fired 500lb shells which they have. At any rate, I guarantee that no troops in houses could stay a moment longer than necessary - as soon as we were out the Germans were in and then they got it badly from our guns.

Further on our right they tried to follow us up but lost somewhat heavily and retired, so here we are again in trenches and again living much the same life as we did at the Aisne only with much less liberty, for the enemy are within 100 yards of us and we cannot move during the day except those of us that have the cover of a large bank which gives us a walk of 150 by 10 yards.

From the Frontline of History

There is a big din going on all around as I write from artillery fire, how they manage to carry about enough ammunition is always somewhat of a mystery. Fighting is incessant and so intense that someone must give way before long and I cannot believe if the war continues as fiercely as it is now being waged that it can last for very long.

On the 28 October[88], he writes to another unnamed recipient, again going over the events of the previous days:

I wonder whether the Swinedogs will give me the time to finish a letter straight through even a short one, for I cannot yet send a full account. In a few days I hope to, for our experiences have been unique almost.

On 21st we were ordered (the regiment) to push forward into and through a village of some 2,000 inhabitants. After taking a few houses, one Company most gallantly charged the trenches killing and capturing every man therein. Then proceeded to get more houses and that was where poor ……. was killed.

By the evening we had captured a large brewery and next day I commanded two Companies and we took more houses at night. All went well for a few days, although we lost and caused loss a good deal from shooting through loopholes (the Germans had some jolly good

---

[88] Danny Archive: ACC 5653/2/15

shots), and also we got a bad time from the enemy's high explosive shells fired into the brewery.

Then the day before yesterday the devils got busy at us with one of their siege guns. It threw a huge projectile high up into the air as plainly visible as a high cock pheasant then it dwelt at the end of its flight and came down in an aimless way on its side, head or base and the explosion – whew – terrific.

We had to go – we did it very slowly and leisurely, the enemy sniping us from 200 yards - and took up where we are now 200 yards back in trenches with the enemy in the brewery 200 yards away, in houses and just in front in trenches 100 yards off.

We've rather chucked sniping each other. I think we are a bit up at that game, but I don't know what the next move will be – we must wait and see. War now is so scientific and on such a scale one cannot 'go' at each other like the good old days.

Someone sent me a waterproof – I suspect Father – and many, many thanks – it got left two days ago and keeps a German dry now, but I may get it back, and I have just got a Burberry, so am all right. We've had a very hard week – in work, in watchfulness and in fighting but we are all very well and have done very well.

The 26 October is also described in detail in the Battalion War Diary and it ended up being the bloodiest day for the Seaforths so far since the start of the war, with 23 men killed, three missing and 37 wounded:

> *About 6 a.m. a report was heard and a large shell was observed to drop into a building in the brewery. It did not burst and on being searched for was found in an outhouse. It measured 3ft by 3ft 6 ins in length and was about 11 inches across the base. Very shortly afterwards another dropped and burst with great effect demolishing a house. The shell could be distinctly seen in the air and was apparently fired from very close range; it did not fly point forwards, but anyhow sometimes landing on its base and sometimes on its side. As it appeared useless to remain in buildings, the men were ordered into the trenches and the shelling continued for some two hours doing great damage whenever the shells fell in buildings. The houses east of the road also received some attention.*
>
> *As our orders to capture the town and bridge had been cancelled and it appeared quite useless attempting to hold houses if shelled by such big guns, it was decided to retire to the line of the old German trenches (now occupied by A Coy). The retirement was effected and the trenches were extended to the left towards the river. C Coy was sent back to the trenches near Le Ruage (originally occupied by us). They experienced considerable difficulty in getting there coming under shrapnel, Maxim and rifle fire and having to crawl down a very wet ditch. They got back about midday to the position and remained there as reserve. D Coy*

commenced digging in on West side of road and B on east up to 'German' trenches. Before they had got much cover the enemy developed considerable rifle and machine gun fire on our line & reoccupied the Brewery and other houses. This was about 10 a.m. They also opened up with artillery and maxims on the houses in our rear. Our artillery supported us. The enemy did not attempt to attack except a few men who advanced across the open and were nearly all killed. We incurred a good many casualties owing to the lack of cover on the left of our line and to a small trench being enfiladed from the Brewery.

After about 12.30 p.m. the enemy's activity subsided and for the rest of the day we were only bothered by a great deal of sniping. Only ½ of A Coy were in the trenches all day and about ½ of B Coy; the remainder spent the day digging reserve trenches in rear of the bank south of the 'German' trenches.

After dark C Coy was brought up as reserve to D Coy and remained in the trenches already dug in the gardens in rear. Our line was as follows from the right: A Coy in touch with R. Irish Fusiliers, B Coy up to the main road, D Coy up to the river from the main road. Only ½ A Coy and ½ B Coy were in the trenches the remainder being in reserve under cover of the bank. Communication between B and D Coys was interrupted by the main road. During the night the trenches were improved and the position made good.

From the Frontline of History

On the 1 and 2 of November, Teddy was to write the last two letters that have survived[89]. The first was to his sister Elsie. The two armies were now hard up against each other, digging into positions that would barely move until 1917 and the 3rd Battle of Ypres, otherwise known as Passchendaele.

> *We are close up against each other here and both sides dig each other stronger every day, and our wire obstacles will soon touch theirs so that neither side can possibly get at each other. Such is the impasse now in Modern War. I'm very fit and well and we are all terribly keen to get on for we feel we have the Swinedogs very nearly in the potage.*

How wrong he was. The Germans were far from being in the soup and the war would last another four years and claim his and so many other lives in the process. In the final letter, on the 2nd November, Teddy writes to an unnamed family member, possibly his sister Mary, in which he rather plaintively asks for "quite the smallest of sponges" and a nailbrush; trench life was really affecting his spirits, but there was still time for humour as he relates in this letter:

> *I'm getting a crick in the back from running down trenches with my head between my knees. The other day the Dublin Fusiliers had been having a bad time in the trenches and one of the men had had a man killed on either side of him while the next man beyond had been very badly wounded. At the end of the bout of shelling this chap began lighting his pipe and shouting across to his next sound comrade*

---

[89] Both in the Danny Archive: ACC 5653/2/15

remarked "Mick, this Belgian tobacco and damned French matches will be the death of me!"

The Seaforths remained in their position in early November, working on the trenches continually to improve them. Generally, this was done under cover of darkness to help avoid the attention of snipers, but the bright moonlit nights early in the month meant that little work could be done. A detachment of 58 men arrived as reinforcements on the 3 November, but no officers were among them. The Battalion faced a very difficult situation on the night of the 6 November and during the following day when D Company was badly mauled in the Ploegsteert Wood action[90] where Captain Forbes Robertson was killed, Captain Parker (3rd Black Watch) was wounded and missing, and a further seven men killed, 33 men wounded, and six missing – a very heavy toll.

There was regular shelling of their position and with the terrible weather the trenches were in a very poor state. We now have to follow Teddy's progress from the official Battalion War Diary:

Very wet weather with odd day or so of cold and frost. Trenches in an awful state, parapets and traverse falling in and some of the low lying trenches filling with water – mud very bad.[91]..... Very great trouble was experienced in preventing the parapets falling in, both in dry weather and wet. The soil was clay and the men had burrowed under the parapet and it was constantly falling in. We had great trouble with the

---

[90] As Teddy was not involved in that action, I do not cover it in detail here.
[91] 2nd Battalion Seaforth Highlanders War Diary: 12 – 16 November 1914

> drainage which was a very difficult matter. In some places we managed to board in the roadway of the trench but in others boards or bricks that we put in were soon covered with mud.

On 17 November the Seaforths were at last able to hand their trenches over to the Scottish Rifles (19th Battalion) and marched to billets in Pont de Nieppe. Then, on 18 November, the whole Battalion managed to have baths and to be issued with a clean shirt – something that was very much appreciated by the men.

However, the respite was short lived and soon they were back on the frontline, taking over trenches at Douve from the Royal Irish Fusiliers on the 21 November. The weather was freezing cold and it was snowing heavily with hard frosts. This brought its own difficulties, as not only was the ground hard to dig but the newly turned earth would also be visible in the snow and attract artillery and sniper fire. The Battalion War Diary describes the scene:

> An extraordinarily crooked line in places very dangerous as facing each other. Our line extended from River Douve 300 yards south west of La Petite Douve farm to CE of La Chapelle de Notre Dame de Grace. Trenches originally made by French. Enemy about 400 – 500 yards off. Had to lie low all day and could move very little by day as intercommunication so bad and communication to rear non-existent….

Rations had to be carried up to the trenches about 1 ½ miles. Hard frost, very cold[92].

The good news for Teddy was that he was now allowed some leave, the first since he had landed with the British Expeditionary Force in August. It had been three months of relentless privation, fighting and trenchwork, with almost incessant shelling and sniping by the enemy. Even for highly experienced soldiers like Teddy it must have been very debilitating and the opportunity to go on leave would be very welcome.

Inevitably leave was short, and on 1 December Teddy returned to the frontline; but by now he had been promoted to Major, the penultimate promotion of his career.

There must have been a ripple of excitement go through the Battalion, despite the conditions, as on the 3rd December King George V visited the headquarters of the 4th Division and presented decorations to various officers and N.C.Os. Teddy was not one of the few chosen to attend, but would surely have shared in the general sense of gratification and pride.

On 6 December, Teddy had to go to hospital where he stayed for a week before being discharged on 13 December. The effect of trench warfare on his health can be seen in the increasingly regular bouts of sickness he suffers. At 41, he was relatively old for a frontline combat soldier living life in the trenches. His service overseas in India and Africa also seems to have undermined his health

---

[92] 2nd Battalion Seaforth Highlanders War Diary: 22 November 1914

and although he always protested his fitness to his family in letters, and had the physique and training of a sportsman, his relatively weakened state must have meant that he was physically less able to face the challenges of the war than a younger man.

His arrival back from leave was just in time for him to join the Seaforths as they relieved the Irish Fusiliers in the Douve trenches. He was also back in command of A Company, the role of Senior Major being taken by Major Arbuthnot. On 18 December, his birthday, it rained. It must have been difficult to celebrate under such conditions.

On the following day the 'Bulge' in the line that ran through Ploegsteert Wood was attacked by the 11th Brigade. Heavy artillery, rifle and machine gun fire raked the frontline all day. This culminated with an attack at 2.30 p.m. which was not altogether successful on account of the waterlogged state of the terrain, but some ground was made.

The Seaforths were then relived by the Royal Irish Fusiliers and went into billets, returning to the frontline on 23 December in time for one of the most extraordinary moments of the war: the Christmas Truce. The Seaforths had just been reinforced with 71 men and took over from the Royal Irish Fusiliers after dark. It was very cold and wet underfoot and there was some snow during the day. Teddy would have been delighted that Captain Carden, his old polo playing friend and longstanding comrade-in-arms, had returned after recovering from his wound.

On Christmas Eve, everyone's mind would naturally have turned to thoughts of home. While there was some of the usual sniping and shelling by field guns in the day, they did little damage. Like most European nations, the Germans begin their festivities on Christmas Eve and, sure enough, the Germans ceased hostilities after dark and started celebrating with singing and shouting.

The Battalion diary describes the events of that night and the next day:

> *Some of our men went right up to their trenches and obtained a certain amount of information. We put up a lot of wire during the night.*
>
> *25th December*
>
> *Hard frost, misty. Not a shot fired and we were able to walk about in the open even after the mist rose. Had some trouble keeping the Germans away from our line. Put some more wire out and did a good deal of work by day.*

As we can read, it is quite a contrast to the romantic picture that has been painted in the media, and which has become a trope for our shared common humanity. The famous account[93] of the Scottish kilted regiment that played football with the Germans was for a long time, erroneously, thought to have been the Seaforths. It is now clear that this was a case of mistaken identity,

---

[93] Oberstleutnant Johannes Niemann of the German 133 Royal Saxon regiment (133/Saxons) in the 1968 BBC radio documentary *Christmas Day Passed Quietly*

and that it was actually the 2nd Battalion of the Argyll and Sutherland Highlanders.

There are accounts of socialising, such as that of Corporal John Ferguson of the Second Seaforth Highlanders[94]:

> *What a sight - little groups of Germans and British extending almost the length of our front! Out of the darkness we could hear laughter and see lighted matches, a German lighting a Scotchman's cigarette and vice versa, exchanging cigarettes and souvenirs.*

But in a letter written by Major J. V. P. Hawksley, who was serving with the Royal Warwickshire Regiment, and is dated December 27, 1914, he states:

> *The Seaforths ... would have none of it and when the Germans in front of them tried to fraternise and leave their trenches, the Seaforths warned them that they would shoot.*[95]

Far from embracing the enemy, the Seaforths wanted nothing to do with them. One cannot imagine that Teddy would have tolerated such fraternising, not from any lack of empathy, but because of all the blood that had been spilled already. The Seaforths were happy enough to refrain from shooting at the Germans and instead use the time to improve their defences, an activity that

---

[94] https://www.theweek.co.uk/world-news/first-world-war/61816/wwi-christmas-truce-soldiers-memories-of-the-brief-peace

[95] Reproduced from letters to be auctioned - https://www.thetimes.co.uk/article/scottish-regiment-that-refused-to-play-ball-in-christmas-truce-09qbs85vll9

would normally be impossible in daylight. As to playing football, that would be going too far.

As 1914 ended, it must have dashed the hopes of those who had thought it would all be over by Christmas. The fighting had rapidly turned from the hectic fast-moving assault – surely a blitzkrieg before Hitler's adoption of the word – of the opening weeks, into a static bloody, mud-bound war of attrition. The last few days of December 1914 were bitterly cold, with hard frost, gales and torrential rain, no time to be out in the open, especially if your health was weak.

The Seaforths took over the trenches from the Royal Irish Fusiliers from the 31 December to the 4 January. It was relentless and miserable:

> *Very wet tour – rained nearly every night and part of every day. Ground in a very sodden state and water rising in the trenches in some places despite constant pumping, bailing and draining. Wire improved and new machine gun emplacement made on right and left flanks. A lot of shelling by heavy, medium and light guns. Small field guns bothered us considerably, causing several casualties and damaging trenches and parapets a good deal.*[96]

Teddy only made it as far as 2 January before coming down with severe influenza and he was sent to Queen Alexandra's Military Hospital on Millbank in London. He was treated here for six days before being discharged on 11

---

[96] 2nd Battalion Seaforth Highlanders Battalion War Diary

January[97]. He did not return to the trenches until 20 February. That his recuperation took such a long time, at a moment when the army was so overstretched, and despite his indefatigable commitment, shows that he must have been seriously ill. This was, after all, at a time when influenza could more often prove fatal than today – as the world would discover at the cost of millions of lives just three years later.

It was at this moment that his contribution was officially recognised and, along with several fellow Seaforths, he was mentioned in the despatches of Field Marshal Sir John French, (Commander-in-Chief of the British Expeditionary Force at that time), for gallant and distinguished service in the field.

After recovering, Teddy returned to the front, finding that in many ways he had not missed much. The Battalion was still manning the Douve trenches, the enemy were still sniping, and shelling and the weather was still miserably wet and cold. On his return, the 10th Canadian Infantry were attached to the Brigade for training and Teddy was posted to them as their liaison officer, sharing his experience of many months of trench fighting.

Between the 6-9 March the Seaforths were back on the frontline in the trenches. The weather was at first wet, before turning to snow and finally to frost. The trenches needed continual maintenance, but the moon was rising

---

[97] The "missing" three days presumably being accounted for by travel from the front back to London

very late which meant that it was difficult to work through the night – the threat from enemy snipers was ever present.

There was some cheering news though on 10 and 11 March, when the Seaforths heard of the success of the 1st Battalion Seaforth Highlanders at Neuve Chapelle, where they had advanced after a tremendous artillery bombardment – described as "over a thousand shells a minute, and it must have been that[98]" – and captured the German trenches.

For a few days in mid-March, it appeared that they were going to be transferred close to their old position from the previous October. But in the end, they were sent back to the Douve trenches, where the Brigade line was being readjusted. They had to give up their trenches to 7th Argyll and Sutherland Highlanders and instead take over those previously occupied by 1st Royal Warwickshire Regiment[99] north of the Douve river. Teddy was commanding A Company on the right centre of the firing line east of the Messines road. The Battalion War Diary describes the conditions:

> *The new trench when taken over was found in a very bad sanitary state, it had practically no wire in front and was quite unprotected on left flank as the next portion of trench (held by Royal Warwickshire Regiment) formed a step 200 yards in echelon to the rear. The trench is only about 150-200 yards from La Petite Douve farm held by the enemy and is exposed to enfilade and long range reverse fire from the*

---

[98] http://www.scotlandswar.co.uk/pdf_Neuve_Chapelle.pdf
[99] 14th Brigade of 5th Division

left. The accommodation for the men was bad. During our tour wire was put out all along the front and a hedge running down from the enemy on the left was well wired. Dug outs were made and a good many improvements effected.

Weather was rather wet – April weather – heavy storms of rain and bright intervals. One very bad night - quite a useful moon and not too much. With the exception of a good deal of shelling on the 23rd all along the line and rather heavy sniping at dusk and dawn daily, there was not much activity on the enemy's part. We did a considerable amount of patrolling every night and got a certain amount of useful information.

The condition of the trenches meant that maintenance work was continual and new breastworks were started to join up with the neighbouring trench held by the Royal Warwicks. However, this work had to stop on 31 March due to heavy sniping. Some casualties were also resulted from enfilade sniping and reverse long range shots on the left, something that continued over the next few days – reflecting the poor siting and exposed position of the trench. When work recommenced during the night of the 1 April, the Germans responded by shelling the working party, as well as by raking the line with machine gun fire, fortunately without success. Aside from being April Fool's Day (although for once one cannot imagine Teddy felt like making anyone a Fool), 1 April was also Bismark's birthday, and the Germans put up red flares all night. The Battalion's first case of measles – a highly contagious disease that could spread very rapidly if left unchecked – was also noted that day.

Teddy's time at Douve was coming to an end though, however, and he managed to guide A Company through their final days in these trenches without any further casualties, although D Company was not so fortunate losing several men to sniping.

The Battalion then marched to Bailleul to the South West of Ypres, where they spend the next ten days recovering and preparing for their next posting. The weather was fine, and it must have been a very welcome pause in the hostilities, except for the night of the 13/14 April when a Zeppelin bombed Bailleul. War from the air was still a new and terrifying threat.

Chapter 12 The Second Battle of Ypres

On the 22 April, the Germans released 160 tonnes of chlorine gas onto the French, French Colonial forces, and Canadian regiments facing them. This was the first ever use of poison gas in wartime. The resulting massacre of 6,000 men opened up a large gap in the Allied lines through which the Germans poured in a rare offensive attempting to seize the road to Calais. The Second Battle of Ypres had begun.

The action was described in the Scotsman[100]:

> *At five o clock in the afternoon a plan carefully prepared was put into execution against our French Allies on the left. Asphyxiating gas of great intensity was projected into their trenches, probably by means of force pumps and pipes laid under the parapets. The fumes, aided by a favourable wind, floated backwards, poisoning and disabling over an extended area those who fell under their effect. The result was that the French were compelled to give ground for a considerable distance.*

In response, in the early morning of the 25 April, the Seaforths were moved into position near Wieltje, just outside Ypres to the north east, ahead of a planned attack on St Julien. The Brigade disposition from left to right was: Royal Warwickshire Regiment – Seaforth Highlanders – Royal Dublin Fusiliers

---

[100] The Scotsman - 1 May 1915

From the Frontline of History

– Royal Irish Fusiliers. We must turn again to the Seaforths' Battalion War Diary which gives a detailed eyewitness account of the fighting that day. As usual, Teddy is commanding A Company:

Title - *Further account of action on 25th April 1915*

Notes in margins - Reference Map – Belgium, sheet 28 N.W.; Times in some cases only approximate

1.15am – Battalion (2nd in Brigade) halted with Brigade. Head of Brigade at Wieltje (square C.28.b) crossroads. Pouring with rain.

1.15am to 2.25am – G.O.C. giving instructions and final orders to CO's in a ruined house in Wieltje. Wieltje in ruins, but luckily all quiet now – houses smouldering still. Very difficult to get information of situation – [as orders were being dictated, staff officers of Canadian Division were coming in to give what information they could, but they had little definite knowledge of the exact situation], and in the end it was not definitely established whether St Julien itself was partially held by us or not. It was known that the Germans had pushed back the French south of Pilckem (square C.2.c) and had crossed the canal near and north of Boesinghe (C.5.d), and further that this line ran roughly from St Julien (square C.12.c) to this place if not further south.

The final orders received were that

1) The 1st Warwicks should attack the wood west of St Julien, which was stated to be held by the Germans.

2) 2nd Seaforth Highlanders should attack on the line between the wood and St Julien – both above to deploy west of St Julien road

3) 2nd Dublin Fusiliers should attack St Julien deploying east of road

4) 1st Irish Fusiliers should attack St Julien on right of Dublin Fusiliers from direction of Fortuin (C.18.c) clearing that place if occupied

5) 7th Argyll & Sutherland Highlanders should be in support behind 1st R. Warwicks

Various other Battns and portions of Battns were placed under Genl [Hull's?] command and some artillery. As far as we could tell most of the other Battns did not report in time, though certain detachments cooperated on our right.

6) The field artillery were ordered to shrapnel the wood W. of St Julien and the howitzers to shell the N.E. of St Julien itself with Lyddite

7) Our object was to occupy the whole of the wood if possible, and St Julien

8) All infantry were ordered to get through the gaps in the wire in front of our old 2nd line (G.H.Q. line) before light, to deploy for action and attack at 4am

2.30am – Started issuing tools etc. and making arrangements. The Battn had been all this time in the pouring rain, which was rather less heavy now. Day was showing signs of breaking now, and it was all important to get through the wire before light. Very little opportunity to give proper orders to Coy commanders.

3.15am – Moved forward – almost light before we got through the gap

3.45am – Received orders to delay attack till 5am as other Battns could not be ready by 4am. The Battn was then advancing with 2 Coys – B & C front, and A & D Coys in rear to position for deployment. Owing to Warwicks being in front drawing fire, we also came under fire almost as soon as we were through the wire.

4am - The fire became quite hot and the order to postpone the attack till 5am came rather late. The Coys had to continue advancing so as to get to some sort of cover as heavy machine gun or rifle fire was now opened, and we were losing considerably.

4.30am – The leading Coys had advanced almost level with farm (in C.17.a) and in the right further still, but further advance was impossible owing to the severe machine gun fire directed on us from the farm in C.16.b and C.17.a

5.30am – Heavy artillery fire was opened on us with considerable accuracy. About this time (or perhaps some time later) the Battns on our right meeting a heavy fire fell back. At the same time and in consequence of this the Battn on our left also fell back some distance. This left the Battn right out by itself and we withdrew to a line of hedge which gave us some cover from 100 to 200 yards in rear. We were still some distance in front of the rest of the Brigade, and shortly after they came back again like a wave. There was no apparent reason why they should have gone so far back – probably some mistaken order.

7am - From this time forward we attempted no further attack having lost very heavily. The Germans were much quieter and hardly shot at us when we moved about. We were able to get a lot of the wounded back to the dressing station in farm C.23.a North.

8.30am – We filled up a gap by throwing 2 sections over the road to the East by Vanheule (C.17.d) farm and increasing the garrison of the farm. After this we started to reorganize and to dig ourselves in behind the hedge running West from Vanheule farm to point in the field 300 N.E. of Shelltrap farm (C.22.b). During the rest of the day there was very heavy shelling of Shelltrap and Vanheule farms, and the line in both sides of us, and in rear of us. The Wieltje-St Julien road was shelled all day. Heavy shell fire all over the slope behind us and into Ypres which continued all night. During the advance we had lost nearly all our tools. At dusk we first of all reorganized companies, then collected tools and started digging in, and by morning had quite a good line of trenches. We gave up Vanheule farm to the Dublin Fusiliers.

This account while vivid does little to convey the sheer lunacy of advancing across open country towards an entrenched German position. Here the same scene is described in the Dundee Courier[101]:

> Then came the order to advance, the point aimed at being some 1,500 yards off. The 7th Argylls, the Seaforths, the Royal, Irish Rifles, the Dublin Fusiliers, and the Warwickshires attacked in company. A terrific storm of shell and rifle bullets swept the country they were advancing over, and the troops suffered heavily.

It was succinctly summarised by Seaforth Private Rattray in the same publication: "*It's pure murder at Ypres*"

We get a further brief insight into the events of the 25 April when Teddy writes to the father of one of his officers who died during the battle[102]:

> The Rev. A. Cameron, Tain, received Saturday the following particulars concerning the death of his son, Lieutenant Ian Cameron, 2nd Seaforth Highlanders, from Major Campion:— On 25th April we were attacking German trenches and a farm house near St Julien. Your son was with my company, and had just taken his platoon on, under a heavy fire, to try push the attack in, and at that time I said to the Commanding Officer how splendidly your son was doing. He was hit, and died of his wounds shortly afterwards, but the doctor assures me he suffered no

---

[101] Dundee Courier - Friday 07 May 1915
[102] Reproduced in the Aberdeen Press and Journal, 11 May 1915

> pain. He is buried near a farm house on the west side of the road, just north of the village of Wieltje, on the Ypres-St Julien road. In offering you my deepest sympathy, I can only tell you of the very excellent manner in which he met his death, and how well he has done out here during the war. He has laid down his life a gallant man and brave soldier.

The casualties were horrific: ten officers were killed or missing with a further nine wounded – nearly two thirds of the total. Other ranks saw 90 killed or missing and 239 wounded – over a third of the Battalion. Lt Col R.S. Vandeleur C.M.G, who was commanding the Battalion, was himself wounded on the 25, and Major K.W. Arbuthnot, the senior Major was killed. A great sadness for Teddy was that one of his longest standing friends, Captain Kenneth MacLachlan, with whom he had had so much success in the Seaforths' polo team, was fatally wounded, dying four days later on the 29 April. Teddy was now the most senior surviving officer and so he assumed command of the Battalion.

H.H.E. Craster describes the casualties in the Scottish Historical review[103]:

> Their casualty list was 50 percent higher than on the day the Highland Brigade was mown down at Magersfontein. It was more than double

---

[103] Scottish Historical Review – The Seaforth Highlanders, August 1914 to April 1916, H.H.E. Craster

the losses which they had suffered at Paardeberg, although that battle produced the heaviest casualty list in the South African War.

Miraculously, Teddy had survived this annihilation, but how much longer would his luck hold?

The next few days were murderous with no respite from the assault by the Germans. On 26 April, the Battalion suffered a further 96 casualties. Understandably, the Battalion Diary is extremely brief on these later dates, since there was no one available to maintain anything more than the briefest record. If the Seaforths thought that the worst might now be over, they were to be proved tragically wrong, and on 2 May 1915 they suffered their first encounter with poison gas in an attack that would later lead to Teddy's death.

On 2 May, at around 5.30 p.m., the Germans sent over a cloud of chlorine gas, after which they attacked. This was the same technique they had used against the French and Canadians – first they used gas to poison or incapacitate the enemy, and they then pressed home their attack once the clouds of gas had dispersed. Knowing that this incursion could be disastrous, Teddy commanded the Battalion to stand firm and repulse the attack.

An eyewitness account by a wounded Seaforth Highlander was reproduced in the Dundee Evening Telegraph[104], and not only relates the terrifying approach

---

[104] Dundee Evening Telegraph - Wednesday 12 May 1915

of this new weapon, but also an incident in which the Germans masqueraded in kilts they had stolen from Canadian troops to approach the British line:

GERMANS IN THE KILT. Fire a Last and Fatal Volley.

During the recent fighting at St Julien the Seaforth Highlanders had their first experience of asphyxiating gas, and one soldier, who is at present recovering from its effects in Glasgow, remarked, in the course of an interview with the Glasgow Herald, the regiment would rather come through three charges than be compelled to lie and wait on the vapour floating over them.

At St Julien the British troops made a strenuous fight, and despite the fact that many were rendered unconscious by the gas, the Germans were unable to occupy the position which was ultimately made secure for the Allies by the Canadians. The first indication, said the soldier, of anything out of the common being employed by the Germans was the effect produced by several heavy shells which burst in the British trenches.

The effect, was similar to the indiscriminate scattering of pepper, and the soldiers suffered severely from smarting of the eyes. Deeming the worst to be over, they settled down comfortably in their dug-outs when someone called attention to the fact that a number of Germans were continually passing along the tops of their trenches. So unusual was the occurrence that our men refrained from firing in the hope of being able to find out what the movements meant. The enemy suddenly disappeared, and a few moments later a greyish green vapour commenced to drift towards the British lines. The soldiers watched, fascinated. Covering a space of 300 yards, the vapour crept slowly onwards, and even small holes and ruts in the ground were filled up.

An officer who had been closely observing the mist quickly exclaimed —"Boys, it is gas of some sort, but you had better lie in the trenches than rise and run the risk being sniped." The men began to pour hot fire into the German lines, which was supplemented by heavy artillery. After a short time the fumes reached the British trenches, and in a matter of seconds groans and coughing, intermingled with curses, indicated the effect of the new German move. Still the soldiers continued to fire, and all at once the Germans in the first lines of trenches left cover and retired rapidly. Some of the gas which had been caught on an eddy of wind had apparently found its way back to the Germans, and, hoisted on their own petard, they made no bones about scurrying to safer positions. The Britons, some of whom were half unconscious, retained sufficient presence of mind to pull the triggers of their rifles as hard as they could, and few of the enemy succeeded in escaping.

About the same time a number men dressed in the Canadians' kilts and jackets advanced towards the British lines. Thinking that they were some prisoners that had escaped, the Seaforths ceased firing, whereupon 'the kilties' dropped upon their knees and poured in a heavy

> volley which found several victims. "But their one volley was their last," was the significant remark from the Seaforth. Later the narrator became unconscious and awakened 24 hours later with splitting headache and general physical weakness which necessitated his removal to the base hospital and thence Scotland. In conclusion, the soldier said that the Allies were dead set upon paying back to the full these inhuman acts.

The Battalion War Diary has a brief entry describing the event:

> About 5.30pm gas sent over. The Battalion stood firm and held their trenches though nearly every man was badly affected. The Battalion on our left had to leave their trenches which were reoccupied by 7th Argyll & Sutherland Highlanders who had to charge through the gas….. The Germans formed up ready for an attack but we inflicted losses on them and it came to nothing. For several days the men were dropping off sick. Some lasted 3 or 4 days and in the case of officers up to a week before they went off sick.

It is these later notes which reveal the true impact of the gas attack. While only relatively few men were killed or wounded on 2 May itself (one man killed, 10 wounded), by 3 May the gas was having a devastating impact, with 24 dead from gas, 324 sick from gas, not to mention 10 other casualties. This was combined with a ferocious bombardment, which commenced at 3.30 a.m. and did not cease for four and a half hours, setting the dressing station on fire. This was too much for anyone to withstand, and the Battalion received orders to abandon the frontline and retire to a deeper position.

This seems to have been the first time that poison gas was used against British troops. As we have seen, Canadian forces had already been hit hard, as had the French and their Colonial forces, but this was the first time British soldiers had faced this indiscriminate killer. The effect of chlorine gas[105] is described as follows:

> *Chlorine was eventually chosen, for a number of key reasons. Chlorine is two and a half times denser than air so it stays close to the ground when released and it also sinks into trenches, shell holes and bunkers....Chlorine gas also disperses over a reasonably short time to safe levels, enabling assaulting troops to safely occupy the gassed area. A disadvantage was that chlorine is one of the few coloured gases so it can be seen.*

> *British Sergeant Elmer Cotton wrote a description of men who had been gassed by chlorine in his diary: "their colour was black, green and blue, tongues hanging out and eyes staring... some were coughing up green froth from their lungs". Chlorine gas is fatal in a few minutes at a concentration of 1,000 parts per million (ppm) and 400 ppm is fatal if exposure is for more than 30 minutes.*

---

[105] A. P. Padley - https://journals.sagepub.com/doi/pdf/10.1177/0310057X1604401S05

Chlorine is highly corrosive and kills by destroying lung tissue probably by forming hydrochloric acid when dissolved in lung fluid. Lung irritation was severe, described by one survivor as like having lungs filled with red hot needles.

Pulmonary oedema and acute respiratory distress syndrome could follow gassing. Eye and skin irritation also occurred. Sir Arthur Hurst, a physician who had an interest in gas injuries, estimated that of the soldiers without protection that survived gassing long enough to reach a clearing station, about 5% would die within 48 hours.

Of those that survived to reach a base hospital, Hurst calculated about 1-2% died by the second or third week, usually from broncho-pneumonia or other pulmonary complications. Survivors of chlorine gassing would return to the frontline after an average of 60 days convalescence.

Teddy was gassed on 2 May but stayed at his post until 6 May, unquestionably causing severe damage to his health while he did so. Why did he do this? He must have known the impact it was having on him. The reality is that, if one looks at the roll of officers for May, there were almost no experienced soldiers left. Between the 25 April and the 8 May, the Battalion had had 28 of its 36 officers killed, wounded or gassed[106]. The most senior officer was Capt J.O.

---

[106] It is worth reflecting on the slaughter of this period for a moment, as one can feel that the numbers become almost meaningless they are so large. In one month between the 25th April and 24th May the Battalion lost 1,000 Officers and Men in casualties. That is like wiping out an entire Battalion, every single man, in one month.

Hopkinson who took over command when Teddy was hospitalised; he was the only Captain left. There was only one Lieutenant, Lieut D. Munro (Lieut MacWatt, the Adjutant between the 1 – 8 May, was hospitalised with gas on the 8 May). The rest were 2nd Lieutenants, the most junior of the officer ranks, whose experience might be measured in days rather than months or years. There was literally no one else left to try and organise the retreat of the Battalion. This surely explains why Teddy continued in his post until reinforcements might arrive. His commitment to duty almost certainly cost him his life as the corrosive effect of the gas went untreated.

There is a poignant note at the end of the War Diary's May entry:

> *On 2nd May our respirators were found to be no good being made of nothing but woollen waistbelts*

His family were unquestionably very concerned and the only letter we have of these final months is from his sister Mary to her and Teddy's uncle Walter[107]:

> *We are uneasy about Teddy. He had a bad dose of gas last Sunday. He was too busy with his men to look after himself until about Thursday he had to go to hospital Temp 102 – Friday he wrote in train on his way to Boulogne, where I suppose he is now hospitalised. He wrote feeling confident, but one always feel that anything likely to affect his lungs is*

---

[107] Danny Archive: ACC 5653/2/10, dated May 9 [1915]

rather serious, on account of the attack of [Pneumonia? /illegible] which he had in India.

Teddy would remain in Britain convalescing for the next four months, reflecting the seriousness of his condition. Nonetheless, his war was not yet over.

From the Frontline of History

Chapter 13 The Return to the Front

Almost incredibly, Teddy returned to frontline duty on the 11 September 1915 for a short and bitter coda both to his career and his life. Again, one senses that his sense of duty and commitment to his men, combined with the desperate state of the British Army in late 1915, drove him to return to the war when he should rightly have been invalided out. However, he was Lieutenant Colonel of the Battalion now, a position he had worked towards for all of his career, and his men were in a dire state; it was inconceivable that he could simply walk away.

It was at this time that his appointment to the post of temporary Lieutenant Colonel, commanding the Battalion, was also formally Gazetted[108]. He had reached the pinnacle of his career.

The 2nd Battalion Seaforth Highlanders had been transferred from the battlefield of Ypres and were occupying trenches near Toutvent, east of Acheux, north of Amiens. Initially the area was quiet, but in October German activity intensified. On 2 October there was a short but ferocious bombardment where up to 100 4.2" high velocity Howitzer shells fell on the Battalion's position in 45 minutes, temporarily burying three men and damaging the trenches. The Germans also fired rifle grenades, wounding two

---

[108] 18 October 1915, page 10245 – 'Seaforth Highlanders (Ross-shire Buff's, The Duke of Albany's) Major E Campion to be temporary Lieut-Colonel. Dated 29th September 1915

men, but were silenced when the Seaforths returned their own grenades using a catapult.

The War Diary now has an almost insouciant tone, after all that the men had witnessed it would take extraordinary events to evince much passion. In mid-October we read of hand-to-hand combat in the British trenches:

> The enemy showed some activity in patrolling & on two occasions they bombed one of our listening posts. In the battalion on our right, one German got into their front trench and killed one man and wounded two and then made his escape. Nothing of much interest occurred. Germans were working fairly constantly and at times were stopped by our machine gun fire. There was a certain amount of intermittent shelling which did no serious harm. A few rifle grenades were thrown at us.
>
> 18th October
>
> Enemy shelled the whole line on and off throughout the day. The fire was particularly heavy on the left Coy. Frontline communications trenches and support line were shelled. Shelling started at 8.30 am and continued intermittently until dusk. Some quite heavy guns were used and heavy trench mortars. Evidently some new guns had been brought up. Considering the nature of the bombardment surprisingly few casualties were caused which speaks well of the state of the trenches now. A good deal of the parapet and traverses especially on the left

were rather seriously damaged. Precautions were taken in case this was preparatory to an attack but the night passed very quietly. Our artillery replied but only slightly.

One point of interest was that on the 25 October, there was another troop inspection by King George V, the Prince of Wales and the French President Poincaré, and M Millerand (French War Office Minister) in Acheux. We have no record of Teddy attending, but, as the Commanding Officer of the Battalion, it is entirely possible.

By the end of the month, the fighting strength of the Battalion is noted as having decreased from 24 officers and 901 men at the beginning to 22 Officers and 825 men.

If the Germans were relatively quiet at this time, the biggest enemy that Teddy had to confront was the weather and the terrain which was causing severe damage to the trenches on which the troops depended for their lives:

> Very bad day of steady heavy rain. Rained all day practically without stopping and after a pause most of the night as well. Trenches falling in everywhere in an almost incredible way. Many of the trenches getting very bad, parapets falling in and filling the trench with mud. Very difficult to deal with.[109]

---

[109] 2nd Seaforths War Diary 2 November 1915

From the Frontline of History

Only on the 3 November did it stop raining, but the improved visibility meant that the Germans could now shell the British lines causing further damage and eight casualties.

One of the final entries in the diary while the Battalion was under Teddy's command deals with the work the Battalion had to do on their trenches. As a highly experienced officer who had been fighting on the Western Front for over a year, he would have understood the importance of proper trench construction better than anyone. Most of the other officers were now so new to the front that they would have unquestionably benefitted from his experience in directing the work that was needed to prepare the trenches properly. In the War Diary[110] there is a description of the work needed:

> *The trenches were in a shocking state, most of the dug outs have collapsed except the German deep ones. Traverses have fallen in and also sides of trenches. The bottom of trenches much used have become filled with thick mud. The left Coy is particularly bad. The trench is passable by day and can only be held in parts. The centre Coy was fair and the Right Coy after a couple of day's work was not too bad. The left of the support line (Rob Roy) was nearly impassable and remained so. The reserve line has collapsed very badly and will doubtless continue to do so being an old converted German trench.*

---

[110] 2nd Seaforths War Diary 15 – 21 November 1915

The idea was to hold the left Coy at its worst bits by posts with the men living in dugouts in Jones trench (support). During the tour we concentrated our work on this trench, so as to make it possible to live there without destroying it. The trench is not complete as a fire trench or as a living trench. It is not revetted nor has it enough fire steps. Dugouts have to be made and trench boards laid down, Drains also require to be dug. Our work was much hindered owing to men working there showing up in the bright moonlight to the Germans against the skyline. They sniped constantly and bothered us with rifle grenades – with considerable success.

Note it is now very obvious to us how many faults have lately been made in digging trenches:

1) Trenches have been dug deep with absolutely straight sides, the earth thrown up has not been kept away from the edge. Consequently in heavy rain the whole thing has collapsed. There should have been a berm of about one yard on the top and the sides should have been sloped.

2) We have been digging too many trenches and have consequently been unable to finish them all off properly. They are not revetted nor have they got footboards. No communication trench with any traffic down it at all will be worth anything unless it is boarded. Even now the boarded CTs are the only ones we can use and they want a lot of attention

3) All fire and service trenches which are much used must be boarded unless they are to be turned into a quagmire.

4) Much very bad sandbag work has been done partly in our efforts to 'save' sandbags. Very large traverses have been cut which have in some cases been revetted by a thin layer of sandbags. If sandbags are used they must be really well laid. One thickness is useless in a big traverse. The weight of water merely bulges them out.

5) Drainage to a certain extent had been thought of but not always and in many cases not at all. The whole question is very difficult because if the trench is not boarded the bottom will be churned up into thick mud and that will not run away.

On 15 November the continual rain turned to snow, and it became very cold. The weather worsened on 16 November with three inches of snow falling, compounded by rain later in the day which froze during the night. On 17 November there is a simple entry:

Lt Col Campion to hospital 17th November. Captain Hopkinson assumed Command

From the Frontline of History

Teddy formally relinquished his post of temporary Lieutenant Colonel on 18 November[111]. It must have been clear that Teddy's combat career was over and he was now fighting for his life.

Teddy was transferred back to Britain, being hospitalised on the 25 November at the Queen Alexandra Military Hospital in London suffering from gastritis. This is a condition in which the stomach lining has been worn away, causing burning pain to the patient. Was this a side effect of the poison gas attack he had suffered, or an infection that he had contracted while at the front? We have no way of knowing. What is certain is that he remained in hospital for a month before being discharged on the 24 December 1915, presumably in order to return home for Christmas – a time of year that he treasured above all others. Perhaps he knew that he was dying, and felt that the inevitable pain was a price worth paying in order to travel down to his family home in Sussex.

Two days later, on Boxing Day, he was readmitted to the Queen Alexandra Hospital where it was found that his gastritis had now evolved into a duodenal ulcer, a condition in which an ulcer drives a hole through the wall of the duodenum (the small intestine) so that any food or stomach acid will leak into the abdomen, causing intense pain. Teddy would not leave hospital again, dying two months later on 25 February 1916. He was 42 years old.

---

[111] 14 February 1916, London Gazette, page 1666 – Seaforth Highlanders (Ross-shire Buff's, The Duke of Albany's) Major Edward Campion relinquishes the temporary rank of Lieutenant-Colonel. Dated 18th November 1915

From the Frontline of History

It is worth considering for a moment Teddy's death and its causes. It is clear that he was badly gassed on the 2/3 May 1915 and that the delay in seeking treatment would have been severely injurious to his health. We know that he had suffered from other serious ailments while in the trenches, such as influenza, and that he had a history of respiratory illness from his time in India. Nonetheless, he was able to recover sufficiently from the gassing to return to the front in September 1915, although his recuperation time was twice the typical period for soldiers affected by gas poisoning. This undoubtedly reflected the seriousness of his injury. Duty called notwithstanding, and after the devastation of the Battalion and the ongoing war of attrition, there was a tremendous need for experienced officers on the frontline. Teddy would surely have felt that call, returning to the trenches to play his part.

When invalided out in November 1915, he was suffering from gastritis, an injury seemingly unrelated to gas poisoning. In the last record we have before his death, this condition has deteriorated to a duodenal ulcer. However, on his military record it states definitively that his death was due to gas poisoning.

How are these seemingly unconnected afflictions related? Having discussed Teddy's case with a number of eminent medical consultants, it has been suggested that stress ulceration may have caused the duodenal ulcer as a consequence of having so much lung damage. Dr Craig Goldsack, of London University Hospital, commented:

> *"Burns victims are very vulnerable to a particular form of duodenal / gastric ulceration called Curling's Ulcer (actually multiple erosions*

rather than a single ulcer). The cause is the massive physiological stress and fluid shifts these patients incur. In victims of chlorine gas exposure, most of the fluid will leak into the lungs (pulmonary oedema). Curling's Ulcers are seen only rarely now because burns patients are treated prophylactically with large doses of anti-ulcer drugs. In this case perhaps there was a grumbling inflammation which flared up during the subsequent stress of returning to the trenches."

From the Frontline of History

'Major of Seaforth Highlanders' from L' Illustration, 19 June 1915

Could it be Teddy?

From the Frontline of History

Teddy's grave, Holy Trinity, Hurstpierpoint, West Sussex

Teddy's medals, sold in 2018

(Noonan's of Mayfair)

From the Frontline of History

Chapter 14 Teddy's Funeral

His funeral is poignantly described in the West Sussex County Times, the local newspaper to his family's home in Hurstpierpoint[112]:

> *DEATH OF MAJOR EDWARD CAMPION. The death has taken place of Major Edward Campion, late of the Seaforth Highlanders, youngest son of Colonel and the Hon. Mrs Campion, of Danny Park, Hurstpierpoint, and grandson of the first Viscount Hampden, who succumbed to the aftereffects of gas poison in the fighting near Ypres nearly a year ago.*
>
> *Born in 1873, Major Campion entered the Army in 1895 and had considerable service in the Egyptian campaign, the South African War, and India….. The late Major Campion had borne many hardships with his battalion, and subsequent to the gas attack which prostrated him, he attained the rank of temporary Lieut. Colonel. He was early mentioned in dispatches. He appeared in the casualty list suffering from gas poisoning 1st June last, and in the summer and autumn last year, when convalescent, spent much time at Danny, where his kindly disposition and characteristic courtesy endeared him to all classes. He made excellent progress and looked forward to re-joining his regiment at the front, but he had a bad relapse which compelled him to undergo*

---

[112] West Sussex County Times, 4 March 1916

medical treatment again, and this renewed illness from the after-effects of the poisoning had a fatal ending on Friday.

The most detailed account of his funeral is related in the Mid Sussex Times[113] and is reproduced in full in the appendix:

For interment Major Campion's remains were conveyed to Hurstpierpoint, arriving there on Sunday evening. They were at once taken to the Parish Church, where they were received at the lychgate by the Rev. M. H. Waller and the Rev. C. H. Piggott (Rector), the latter reading the opening sentences of the Burial Service and a prayer or two. The scene was a solemn one, the only lights in the spacious building being those on the altar, the chancel corona, and four processional candles. With these lights on either side, the coffin, which bore the deceased officer's sword and service cap resting on the glorious pall of the Union Jack, remained in the chancel all night, and for some time watchers were present in the church. ....

....The choral portions of the deeply impressive service were sustained by the combined choirs of Holy Trinity and St. George's Churches, Mr. H. Shepherd being at the organ. The choir procession was headed by the Rev. M. H. Waller, bearing a crucifix, and the Rev. F. G. Finch, and at the rear came the Rev. C. H. Piggott, the Rev. F. H. Campion (brother of the deceased officer), the Rev. W. B. Dunlop (Vicar of Sayers

---

[113] Mid Sussex Times - 29 February 1916

Common) and the Dean of Chichester (the Very Rev. Dr. Hannah). After the singing of a verse of the National Anthem, in which all joined, and the hymn 'Fight the Good Fight,' the 90th Psalm was chanted, and then Dr. Hannah read the appointed lesson. The hymn 'O what the Joy and the Glory must be' followed, and the Dean continued the service. As the coffin was carried out of the chancel, the hymn 'On the Resurrection morning' was sung. The procession passed through the snow-covered churchyard and under a fall of snow to the grave in the enclosure belonging to the Campion family, and here the committal was taken by the Rev. F. H. Campion. Before the large assemblage dispersed the hymn 'Soldiers, who are Christ's below' was finely rendered, and the Rector offered one or two petitions and gave the Benediction. The Royal Field Artillery also fired three volleys.

And a similar piece in the Sussex Agricultural Express[114]:

Throughout Mid-Sussex on Friday there prevailed a very sorrowful feeling in consequence of the news that the honoured Campion family was in mourning, because of the death in London of Major Edward Campion, the third son of Colonel W. H. Campion, C.B. J.P., and the Hon. Mrs. Campion, of Danny, Hurstpierpoint. The deceased officer was in the 2nd Seaforth Highlanders, and was 42 years of age. He took part in Nile Expedition, and was at the battles of Atbara and Khartoum, and also fought in the late South African War, gaining the Queen's Medal

---

[114] Sussex Agricultural Express, 3 March 1916

with five clasps. He also had the Egyptian Medal with two clasps. When he went out to France he exhibited the same bravery that he had displayed on previous campaigns, and was early mentioned in dispatches. Everybody esteemed him because he was both soldier and man. Early in June, his name appeared in the list casualties as suffering from gas poisoning, and when well enough he came to Danny. Here he received a most cordial welcome from everyone, and when in the autumn the Hassocks V.T.C. dinner was held, Major Campion was one of the guests, and the fine patriotic speech delivered evoked the greatest enthusiasm. Major Campion progressed so well that he was looking forward to re-joining his Regiment. But this was not to be. To the sorrow of his family, he had a relapse, and despite the very best of advice and attention, the gallant officer gradually grew worse, his strength weakened, and on Friday the end came, and gently his spirit passed away.

Chapter 15 Epilogue

An extraordinary coda to Teddy's life came in April 1917, nearly two years after the gassing and more than a year after his death, when his father William Henry Campion received a letter from one of Teddy's Non-Commissioned Officers – Sergeant J Adam. The letter, which is preserved in the Danny Archive[115], included an order from Teddy, that Sergeant Adam had felt was of sufficient importance and power that he had kept it through all those years of trench fighting. His letter reads:

Sir.

Pardon me for taking the liberty in writing you. But as I am in possession of a document (Attached) which I consider of great value and interest, same being written at the hand of your late son Lieut. Col E Campion then commanding 2nd Battalion Seaforth Highlanders. This document was passed along the line at a very critical moment, when the Battalion was for the first time experiencing a gas attack lodged by the enemy on the Ypres Salient. Owing to the peculiar circumstances under which this document was written, and in memory of the 'gallant dead', who died at their post through gas poisoning that day, I suggest with your consent that the attached document be preserved and forwarded to 'the Seaforth Highlanders Association Club' Edinburgh

---

[115] Danny Archive - DAN/487, 488

From the Frontline of History

where it may be seen by all 'Seaforths' who knew your gallant son, and by those in future years who join the regiment.

I have the honour to be

Sir

Your obedient servant No 9950 Sergeant J Adam 2nd Battalion Seaforth Highlanders.

The order, on a battered piece of paper that has clearly been passed through many hands, is slightly torn and written in pencil, states:

To O.C. Coy [Officer Commanding Company] and men to see

Remember no Seaforth Highlander ever has left or ever will leave his post.

Whatever damnable engine of war the enemy use the Seaforths will stick it out and will have their reward in killing the enemy.

E. Campion Major Commander 2nd Battalion Seaforth Highlanders

It has the numbers 3.4.15 at the bottom, which is a slight mystery. It would appear to be the date – the 3 April 1915 – but according to the Battalion War Diary nothing happened on that particular date. The order obviously relates to gas, the new and relatively little known weapon, whose first use ever came on the 22 April 1915. Perhaps soldiers on the frontline like Teddy had heard rumours about its devastating effect, even if facts were few?

What we know is that the order was passed along the line and was considered so important that Sergeant Adam not only kept it, but that he kept it through two more years of fighting before passing it to Teddy's father. He said that it was issued in the context of the use of gas for the first time and that can only be the 2/3 May. The emotional impact it had made is tangible and powerful and it was remembered as such by those that had seen it for years afterwards.

Teddy's order to hold the line

East Sussex Brighton and Hove Record Office: DAN 487-488)

Chapter 16 Conclusion

What can Teddy's life teach us – Is there anything that the diaries and letters of a modestly successful soldier from over a century ago tell us today? The days of Empire are gone and the expansionist confidence of Britain in the 1890s is a distant memory. We all know about the horrors of the Great War and the meaningless loss of life. We also know about the indiscriminate cruelty of poison gas, a horror that rapidly saw it banned again[116] after the war, a prohibition that, with a few exceptions, has endured until today. These exceptions are well known, and lie beyond the scope of this book and the expertise of its author.

Teddy undoubtedly came from a privileged background and established family. His childhood might seem idyllic with a much-loved home and plenty of space to grow up and pursue sporting interests. His family had a very strong moral compass, as evidenced by his Mother's relentless good works, and this was a mantle picked up by her children. Duty and hard work were instilled from the earliest age. As a younger son, and neither the 'heir nor the spare', Teddy had no prospect of a share in the family estate; money was always a consideration. He did not go to university, but went straight into the Army, starting in the militia until a commission became available in his father's old regiment. His

---

[116] It had been banned before - Hague Declaration Against the Use of Asphyxiating Gases of 1899 and the Hague Convention of 1907

father had been a successful soldier, surviving the Crimea and the Indian Mutiny, rising to the rank of Colonel - quite a career, and a hard act to follow.

Perhaps Teddy was fortunate in that he was thrown into some interesting situations so early in his service; how would he have turned out if he had had to push paper at Aldershot rather than be on active service? While he complains about the stupidity of certain Commanding Officers in the conduct of the Sudan Campaign, especially in respect of General Gatacre, he generally never bemoans his lot. He is always ready for duty and is unstinting in his service, even when that includes two years in overseas postings without leave – something that few in active service would tolerate today.

He was a joker, clearly charming and good fun to be around. That endeared him to his seniors, such as Egerton or Murray, but also gave him the sense that he wasn't taken seriously and that his career had suffered as a consequence. It seems likely that until the Boer War he had been making strong progress – as he himself acknowledges, six years to achieve the rank of Captain was no mean feat. The slow progress thereafter perhaps speaks more to the relatively peaceful times in the first decade of the 20th century which naturally limited opportunities. The pyramid of military hierarchy narrows sharply at the top, and if there is no turnover – to put it bluntly, due to injury, death or retirement – then there is little opportunity for promotion, especially when the army is relatively small.

Teddy's compensation was several glorious years of sporting endeavour in India, when his Corinthian qualities were well deployed. While we have no first-hand material from this period, it seems pretty clear that he had a wonderful time playing polo and cricket to a high standard for the Regiment and we know of no active military service while he was in India[117]. His return to Britain is again relatively poorly documented, but he seems to have played an important part in the restructuring of the Volunteer and Reserve units of the Seaforth Highlanders, shaping them into the 3rd Battalion. These troops were critical reinforcements when the First World War broke out, as so many of the full time soldiers were all too rapidly killed or injured. By sharing his battle-won experience and helping to shape these men, Teddy played a crucial role in making sure they were trained and prepared.

It is impossible to write about someone like Teddy and not to consider, even if briefly, affairs of the heart. War diaries are perhaps not the best place to look for insight into a man's inner most thoughts and desires, and the traces are fragmentary to say the least. First of all, it is worth stating the facts; he never married and in his diaries, he never refers to a sweetheart or love interest.

He does make some passing comments about women – such as when he writes about having tea at Assouan with the Misses Fraser and how he was "down-hearted at having to say goodbye to all these beautiful Lady friends". Later on in his Sudan diary, he takes several photographs of a strikingly beautiful Sudanese woman who he captions 'Beauty in the Sudan' and in a picture of her next to her hut but he gives the caption 'Beauty - Ravishing beauty and its

---

[117] He just missed out on the Seaforths participation in the campaign against the Mohmands in the North West Frontier in 1908 as he had returned to Britain.

dwelling'. As often with Teddy, it is difficult to tell whether he is being entirely serious. On the one hand, it would have been highly unusual for a man of his class and background to publicly state his attraction to a local black woman. On the other hand, this was his private diary, so presumably he could say whatever he liked and felt.

There are some other insights in a letter from December 1911 that he wrote to Granville Egerton[118] that offer a brief glimpse into his thoughts:

> *When a man grows tired of the professional, he wants to marry and instead of waiting for a darling, who will stir his pulses and stimulate his mind with the glorious love of woman companionship, he just proposes to the first penniless one eyed lass who looks kindly at him and does a little – quite a little - bit of flattering – urgh! I'd sooner **************** than descend to such mediocrity.*

The asterisks show where Egerton saw fit to scribble out the most revealing part of Teddy's note, with Egerton writing the words; Oh Teddy, Teddy! over the top in blue pencil. It is frustrating that we can't see what lies beneath, but what remains gives us a few clues. He is seemingly looking for love rather than just a wife, someone who will "stir his pulses and stimulate his mind". This letter also highlights another recurring theme throughout Teddy's life, namely the importance of, or need for, money. Teddy's means were always limited, and any potential partner's financial independence was therefore important.

---

[118] National War Museum, Egerton Archive M.1994.112.36 - December 27th 1911

He was a good-looking man and an officer in one of the most respected and 'dashing' of the Army's line regiments. Their exotic uniform and pipe bands made the Seaforths an object of interest wherever they went. Teddy was both a sportsman and an experienced, battle hardened soldier from an old and respected family, one might imagine that he would be considered quite a catch. He was also not immune to pressure from his family to find someone and he writes to his Aunt Shay[119] just before the outbreak of the First World War:

> *I ain't yet got a wife which all my relations think to be a necessity for my happiness – praps! But there is still time*

So why did he never find the wife that both family and social expectations seemed to demand?

One part of the answer may lie in his peripatetic career. For the first thirteen years, he was barely ever in Britain, but instead on overseas postings in places where 'suitable' wives were few and far between. As we have seen, he was ambitious and both wanted and needed to get promotion and advancement. Perhaps he felt that he needed to achieve a certain income or position before settling down. It was not at all unusual for serving officers to marry women much younger than themselves. His letters to Egerton in 1911 reveal that this was now a subject on his mind, particularly since at Fort George he was based in one location for the longest period in his career. Given his presence at the

---

[119] Danny Archive: ACC 5653/2/10

glittering events of the Highland season, one can imagine that suitable marriage candidates were suddenly much more available. However, despite being stationed there for four years, it seems that he never found a partner who matched his ideals.

Another possibility is that he was homosexual. He certainly had a very strong and deep relationship with Granville Egerton, with whom he shared a tent in Crete as well as on campaign in Sudan. There is of course, there is no direct evidence that there was any physical relationship between them and given the societal expectations of the time it would have been anathema. But there is one enigmatic reference in one of Egerton's letters to his mother from Sudan where he states:

> I and my two subalterns sleep alongside one another and one of them is continually 'hitting' out at me during the night. One cold night we had to lie literally clasped in each other's arms to try and get warm – he said afterwards that it was all right except that I smelt so damnably of tobacco.[120]

Whether or not the Subaltern that he clasped in his arms all night was Teddy or not, we cannot say. Unquestionably, there was a paternalistic relationship between them: Egerton the older, more experienced man, naturally took his protégé under his wing. Egerton also never married and seems to have treasured his relationship with Teddy, keeping his letters for many decades

---

[120] Egerton Archive - M1994 112.83

after his death. There are also many photographs of Teddy in Egerton's private albums, more than of anyone else, including a number of Teddy swimming naked in Crete and one of him having a bath. These are certainly not sexualised photographs but mere snaps; but the fact of their being taken and preserved maybe tells us something.

In the Egerton Archive, Egerton kept the order book[121] from his time in Crete and later annotated it with some notes on the various figures that feature therein. What is striking is that all of the officers who served with him in Candia in those early days were killed in the Great War: Daniell, Gaisford, Stockwell, Campion.

He writes a moving epitaph on Teddy:

> *Teddy Campion another greatly beloved subaltern of my company in the 72nd, son of Colonel H Campion of Danny Sussex who also served in the Regiment. Teddy died as a Major in 1916 from the effect of gas poisoning on the western front. 'One of the very best'[122] R.I.P.*

With the outbreak of the First World War, the Great War, the War to End All Wars, we are given the privilege of many eyewitness accounts of Teddy's experiences, taking us with him on the shock of the retreat from Le Cateau, into the trenches of the Marne and Aisne, the house to house fighting, and the

---

[121] Egerton Archive - M.1994.112.168
[122] Egerton's emphasis

misery of Ypres. His first-hand accounts help to bring the reality to life, help us to see anew what we think we know so well.

The horror of poison gas, then a shocking novelty, was engendered by the Germans' need to break through the Allied line at any cost. The initial use against the French had in some ways been extraordinarily successful; the Germans killed over 6,000 enemy troops in minutes, clearing five miles of Allied trenches. However, the Germans failed to capitalise on that advantage to take ground, and no one seems to know why. It is speculated that the German soldiers were themselves taken by surprise with the killing power of the gas, horrified by what they saw, and were too shocked to make the necessary progress; or that they were affected by the gas themselves. In any case, when it came to 2-3 May 1915, the Germans were better prepared, and would push home their attack.

Could the Germans have broken through to Calais, cutting the Allied line and severing Britain's access to her supply lines? That was certainly their plan. That it failed was, in part, due to the sacrifice of people like Teddy and the men of the 2nd Battalion Seaforth Highlanders, and their fellow Regiments on the frontline. They held fast in the face of this horror; they held the line.

Teddy stayed at his post for four days, not only making sure the Germans had been repulsed, but also organising the relief of the wounded and gassed and the reconstitution of the Battalion. With a casualty rate of over 100%, someone needed to manage the urgent call for, and disposition of, reinforcements. All the while, the effect of the gas was ravaging his body. That shows an extraordinary commitment to duty and extraordinary leadership. This leadership had inspired his men, undoubtedly at great personal cost to his own health; but he had been willing to stand there with them, shoulder to shoulder, and ultimately to pay with his life. He led by example and the power of this leadership can be seen reflected in the emotions of Sergeant Adams's letter to his father.

From the Frontline of History

Index

A

Aisne, Battle of the, 7, 170, 171, 174, 187, 202, 260
Akrotiri, 41, 42, 45, 46, 48, 57
Aldershot, 33, 36, 100, 104, 106, 109, 255
Atbara, 15, 61, 62, 69, 81, 82, 84, 88, 89, 98, 102, 248

B

Badfontein, 113, 121
Blockhouse, 16, 108, 109, 113, 114, 115, 116, 125, 129
Boer War, 5, 7, 14, 15, 16, 27, 29, 34, 66, 96, 97, 99, 100, 103, 104, 105, 107, 108, 109, 121, 123, 156, 255
Bombay Presidency, 134, 135
Bradford, Lt Col Sir Evelyn, 68, 171, 172
Burghersdorp, 100, 113, 115

C

Cairo, 60, 61, 67, 70, 83, 93, 97, 98, 100, 103, 128, 137, 150
Cameron Highlanders, 64
Campion, Alice or Elsie, 22, 29, 53, 184, 185, 207
Campion, Charles or Charlie, 5, 27, 28, 29, 104, 105, 109, 185
Campion, Frederick, 26
Campion, Gertrude, 23
Campion, Mary, 29, 144, 207, 232
Campion, William Henry, 21, 53, 250
Campion, William Robert "Bill", 26
Candia, 40
Canea, 36, 37, 38, 41, 45, 47, 48, 56, 272
Ceylon Mounted Infantry, 27, 105, 109
Christmas Truce, 18, 211

263

Crete, 7, 14, 15, 32, 34, 36, 37, 38, 39, 41, 43, 45, 47, 48, 49, 50, 59, 70, 84, 92, 108, 109, 112, 188, 259, 260, 268, 270, 271, 272
cricket, 16, 39, 94, 109, 114, 122, 134, 135, 145, 146, 149, 155, 256

D

Dakhila, 50, 82
Daniell, 37, 38, 41, 56, 260
Danny, 5, 14, 21, 22, 24, 27, 52, 113, 134, 136, 174, 181, 184, 190, 191, 196, 198, 203, 207, 232, 246, 248, 250, 258, 260
Darmali, 61, 62, 66, 70, 90, 97
Dervish, 15, 60, 62, 63, 65, 69, 73, 78, 80, 82, 93, 99, 101, 102
Douve, 209, 211, 215, 216, 218

E

Egerton, 5, 14, 32, 33, 34, 36, 37, 38, 40, 41, 42, 43, 45, 46, 47, 48, 49, 56, 57, 60, 63, 64, 66, 69, 70, 80, 81, 87, 92, 96, 103, 104, 106, 146, 147, 148, 172, 178, 255, 257, 258, 259, 260, 268, 269, 270, 271, 272
Egerton, Granville, 42

F

Fort George, 5, 145, 146, 147, 148, 258
Foumis, 48
Frelinghien, 193

G

Gaisford, 38, *42*, *56*, *260*
Gas, 17, 19, 35, 219, 226, 227, 228, 229, 230, 231, 232, 240, 241, 242, 246, 249, 250, 251, 252, 254, 260, 261
Gatacre, General, 62, 70, 95, 96, 255
Gordon, General Charles, 59

I

Imperial Yeomanry, 27, 28, 105, 109
International review (Crete), 44, 45
International Squadron, 37, 39, 43, 45

J

Jameson, 38

K

Kasr El-Nil, 60, 83, 128, 150
Khalifa, Abdullah Ibn-Mohammed, 59, 61, 72, 73, 74, 75, 78, 79, 81, 84, 97, 100, 102, 103
Khartoum, 59, 60, 62, 66, 68, 70, 73, 81, 93, 96, 100, 103, 248, 272
Kitchener, Sirdar Horatio Herbert, 27, 28, 60, 62, 63, 65, 69, 81, 96, 97, 101

L

Le Cateau, Battle of, 5, 17, 157, 158, 170, 179, 260
Lydenburg, 113, 122

M

Mackenzie, Kenneth, 32
Mahmoud, Emir, 61, 62, 63, 64, 65, 81
Malta, 36
Marne, Battle of, 7, 170, 260
Metemma, Battle of, 59, 101
Meteren, Battle of, 188, 190
Mounted Infantry or MI, 105, 106, 109, 121, 125, 126, 127
Mounted Infantry, or MI, 105
Murray, Colonel R.H., 104

N

Nasirabad or Naseerabad, 128, 134, 136, 141
Nile, 60

O

Omdurman, Battle of, 15, 65, 73, 74, 76, 78, 79, 80, 81, 82, 83, 84, 90, 91, 97, 98, 101, 102, 108, 270

P

Polo, 16, 109, 114, 115, 122, 134, 136, 137, 138, 139, 141, 142, 143, 144, 145, 146, 178, 211, 225, 256

Pretoria, 27, 113, 116, 123

R

Royal Sussex Regiment, 21, 26, 27, 31, 104, 174

S

Seymour, Charlotte (Aunt Shay), 155, 190, 258
Shabluka, 72
Slatin Pasha, 60, 81, 96
Stockwell, 38, 42, 56, 171, 189, 260

V

Venezelos, 48

W

Wieltje, 219, 220, 223, 225
Witkliff, 113
Wonderboom, 113, 129, 130

Y

Ypres, Battle of, 6, 7, 18, 144, 188, 207, 218, 219, 223, 224, 225, 234, 246, 250, 261

From the Frontline of History

Bibliography and Primary Sources

Private Collections

Teddy Campion's Sudan Diary

Teddy Campion's Boer War Diary

The Keep, Sussex Archive, Brighton

Letter from Serjeant J Adams to Colonel W H Campion	DAN 487-8
Photograph Album of Members of the Campion Family	DAN 4/3/2225
Letters to Mrs Walter Campion, from her sister and brother in law Gertrude and W.H. Campion from various Nieces and Nephews and Miscellaneous	ACC 5653/10
First World War typescript letters graphically describing action ? by W.R Campion[123]	ACC 5653/15

---

[123] These are actually written by Teddy TO his brother

Egerton Archive, National War Museum, Edinburgh

Part of a collection of papers relating to Major General Granville George Algernon Egerton, C.B., 1895 – 1951 - notebook kept by Egerton with notes on the history of the regiment	M.1994.112.167
Part of a collection of papers relating to Major General Granville George Algernon Egerton, C.B., 1895 – 1951 - album of photographs taken during the British occupation of Crete in 1897	M.1994.112.170
Part of a collection of papers relating to Major General Granville George Algernon Egerton, C.B., 1895 – 1951 - album of photographs taken on the Nile expedition, 1898	M.1994.112.171
Part of a collection of papers relating to Major General Granville George Algernon Egerton, C.B., 1895 – 1951 - letter to mother from Egerton in Sudan, 3 March 1898	M.1994.112.82
Part of a collection of papers relating to Major General Granville George Algernon Egerton, C.B., 1895 – 1951 - letter to mother from Egerton in Sudan, 30 March 1898	M.1994.112.83
Part of a collection of papers relating to Major General Granville George Algernon Egerton, C.B., 1895 – 1951 - letter to mother from Egerton in Sudan, 4 April 1898	M.1994.112.84

Part of a collection of papers relating to Major General Granville George Algernon Egerton, C.B., 1895 – 1951 - letter to mother from Egerton in Sudan, 7 April 1898	M.1994.112.85
Part of a collection of papers relating to Major General Granville George Algernon Egerton, C.B., 1895 – 1951 - letter to mother from Egerton in Sudan, 31 August 1898	M.1994.112.86
Part of a collection of papers relating to Major General Granville George Algernon Egerton, C.B., 1895 – 1951 - book entitled "Sport and Service in the Seaforth Highlanders" by Captain G.W. Anderson, Dingwall, 1898	M.1994.112.88
Part of a collection of papers relating to Major General Granville George Algernon Egerton, C.B., 1895 – 1951 - book entitled "Reminiscences of the 72nd Highlanders" by Egerton, Vol. I 1822 – 1895, unpublished	M.1994.112.92
Part of a collection of papers relating to Major General Granville George Algernon Egerton, C.B., 1895 – 1951 - book entitled "Reminiscences of the 72nd Highlanders" by Egerton, Vol. II 1896 – 1899, unpublished	M.1994.112.93
Part of a collection of papers relating to Major General Granville George Algernon Egerton, C.B., 1895 – 1951 - typed notes regarding Egerton's memorandum on the early days of the British and Egyptian occupation of Sudan	M.1994.112.97

From the Frontline of History

Part of a collection of papers relating to Major General Granville George Algernon Egerton, C.B., 1895 – 1951 - typed memorandum by Egerton on the early days of British and Egyptian occupation of the Sudan, February 1898 – April 1900	M.1994.112.98
Part of a collection of papers relating to Major General Granville George Algernon Egerton, C.B., 1895 – 1951 - manuscript copy of memorandum by Egerton on the early days of British and Egyptian occupation of the Sudan, February 1898 – April 1900	M.1994.112.99
Album of photographs taken during the advance on Omdurman, by Lieutenant Colonel (later Major General) G.G.E. Egerton, 1898	M.1995.111.1
Part of a collection of papers relating to Major General Granville George Algernon Egerton, C.B., 1895 – 1951 - letter to Egerton from Captain E. Campion in France regarding press cuttings, death of a colonel and behaviour of men, 17 September 1914	M.1994.112.24
Part of a collection of papers relating to Major General Granville George Algernon Egerton, C.B., 1895 – 1951 - letter to Egerton from Captain E. Campion in France regarding press cuttings, 25 September 1914	M.1994.112.25
Part of a collection of papers relating to Major General Granville George Algernon Egerton, C.B., 1895 – 1951 - letter to Egerton from Captain E. Campion regarding time in Crete and regimental news, 8 January 1911	M.1994.112.32

From the Frontline of History

Part of a collection of papers relating to Major General Granville George Algernon Egerton, C.B., 1895 – 1951 - letter to Egerton from Captain E. Campion regarding battalion gossip, 9 January 1910	M.1994.112.34
Part of a collection of papers relating to Major General Granville George Algernon Egerton, C.B., 1895 – 1951 - letter to Egerton from Captain E. Campion regarding battalion gossip, 17 March 1911	M.1994.112.35
Part of a collection of papers relating to Major General Granville George Algernon Egerton, C.B., 1895 – 1951 - letter to Egerton from Captain E. Campion regarding mess, battalion gossip and early marriages, 27 December 1911	M.1994.112.36
Part of a collection of papers relating to Major General Granville George Algernon Egerton, C.B., 1895 – 1951 - letter to Egerton from Captain E. Campion regarding promotion, 14 July, possibly 1909	M.1994.112.40
Part of a collection of papers relating to Major General Granville George Algernon Egerton, C.B., 1895 – 1951 - order book belonging to Egerton during the International Occupation of Crete	M.1994.112.168

Templar Study Centre, National Army Museum, London

Bound typescript manuscript cuttings and photograph: Diary of the Detachment, 1st Bn Seaforth Highlanders at Canea, Crete during the early days of the International Occupation, 1897; compiled by Capt G A Egerton.	1968-07-171
Bound typescript manuscript with cuttings and photograph: Diary of the Khartoum Detachment, 1st Bn Seaforth Highlanders, December 1899-March 1900; compiled by Maj G A Egerton; associated with the 2nd Sudan War (1896-1899)	1968-07-172

Bibliography

Queen's Own Highlanders	Lieut-Colonel Angus Fairrie
Queen's Own Highlanders, A Concise History	Trevor Royle
Seaforth Highlanders (Rosshire Buffs, The Duke of Albany's)	Colonel John Sym

About the Author

Nick Bastin is married with three children and lives in London. He has previously co-written A Very Canny Scot, Daniel Campbell of Shawfield and Islay, a biography of one of Scotland's leading figures of the 18th century. He has also written the Black Tower Trilogy – BloodBond, BloodFeud and BloodLine – of alternate reality fiction set in the Highlands and Islands of Scotland.

Printed in Great Britain
by Amazon